Nawal el Sa'adawi is a leading Egyptian feminist, sociologist, medical doctor, novelist and author of the classic work on women in Islam, *The Hidden Face of Eve*. She had a distinguished career in public health, both in Egypt and abroad, until, in 1973, she was dismissed from her post as Director of Health Education in the Ministry of Health in Cairo; and eight years later imprisoned for alleged 'crimes against the State'.

She lives in Cairo with her writer husband; she has a grown-up daughter (also a writer) and a son; and continues to write (she has had 22 books published, several of them now translated into English, including the well loved novel *Woman at Point Zero*) and to campaign internationally for freedom and justice for women and men.

NAWAL EL SA'ADAWI

Memoirs from the Women's Prison

Translated from the Arabic by Marilyn Booth

The Women's Press

First published in English by
The Women's Press Limited 1986
A member of the Namara Group
34 Great Sutton Street, London EC1V 0DX

British Library Cataloguing in Publication Data

el Sa'adawi, Nawal
    Memoirs from the Women's Prison
    1. el Sa'adawi, Nawal   2. Political prisoners—
    Egypt—Biography
    I.Title
    365'.45'0924   HV9843

ISBN 0-7043-4002-X

Typeset by MC Typeset, Chatham, Kent.
Reproduced, printed and bound in Great Britain by
Hazell Watson & Viney Limited,
Member of the BPCC Group,
Aylesbury, Bucks

Dedication

To all who have hated oppression to the point of death,
Who have loved freedom to the point of imprisonment,
And have rejected falsehood to the point of revolution.

To everyone who raised a voice in protest and anger
When they broke down my door by force of arms
And led me to prison on the sixth of September 1981.

To all of those men and women, young people and
    children
Within Egypt and outside
I dedicate this book.

Nawal el Sa'adawi
Cairo
March 1982

Contents

Part I:	The Arrest	1
Part II:	Prison	27
Part III:	Piercing the Blockade	133
Part IV:	Out to the Investigation	142
Part V:	The Death of Sadat	169
Part VI:	The Final Part	195

Part I
The Arrest

I heard a knock at the door.

I was sitting at the small desk in my bedroom, absorbed in writing a new novel. The clock hand pointed to three. It was the afternoon of Sunday, 6 September 1981.

I ignored the knock. Perhaps it was the concierge, or possibly the milkman, or the man who does our ironing. Or it could be anyone else, but if no one were to answer the door, the steps would surely recede.

When I sit down to write, it is the small household tasks, or the sound of the doorbell or telephone, which torture me. I can be rid of the telephone by pulling the cord from the wall, but the door . . . am I to rip the door from the wall?

This novel is tormenting me. I've freed myself completely to write it, letting everything else go for its sake. It's intractable, like unattainable love. It wants me, my entire being, mind and body, and if it can't have that it will not give itself to me at all. It wants all or nothing – it's exactly like me. To the extent that I give to it, it gives to me. It wants no competition for my heart and mind – not that of a husband, nor a son or daughter, nor preoccupation with work of any sort, not even on behalf of the women's cause.

I began working on this novel in the autumn of 1978. At that time, I was in Africa working as a consultant to the United Nations. My home base was Addis Ababa, but my work obliged me to travel frequently from one African nation to another. For the first time in my life, I saw the sources of the Nile in Ethiopia and Uganda. As a child, I had imagined what Lake Victoria must be like; now, its smell and the colour of its water reminded me of Egypt, my homeland, which I carry inside me wherever I go. The streams emerging over the boulders of Ethiopia supply the water for small rivers the colour of the Nile, the tone of my skin. The features of Addis Ababa's inhabitants resemble those of my ancestors, my father and my aunts in the village of Kafr Tahla.

The second knock at the door.

I was still seated, ignoring the knocking, just as I was paying no attention to the car horns from the street below. I've travelled all over the world, but I have never seen the likes of Egyptians for exerting the same pressure with their hands on the car horns as they do with their feet on the accelerator. My flat is on the fifth floor, but the car horns still sound like screams, like a continuous wailing.

My flat in Addis Ababa, which overlooked foothills of green, was a quiet place, one of utter tranquillity, unbroken by voices or car horns. But still the novel spurned and resisted me. I could write scientific studies, draft agreements, write books on women's issues – everything except the novel, this particular novel. It is a strange business: the more I distance myself from Egypt, the further the novel travels from me. No sooner do I land at Cairo Airport, and breathe in the odours of dust and people's sweat, the car horns and pale, fly-laden children's faces, the queues of women in their black *gallabiyyas*,[1] and the broken, exhausted eyes of the men, than the novel comes ever nearer.

I was searching for a writer who has written a great work of literature while absent from the homeland. My mind would tell me it was possible, and I would travel.

I did not travel by choice: I was looking for another homeland. Since the winter of 1972, I had been feeling estranged in my own country. Why? Because I had written a book containing new ideas and because in one of the lectures I gave in the College of Medicine at Ain Shams University in Cairo, I had stood up and given my views on women, society, medicine, literature and politics – for I don't isolate any one of these topics from the others.

I have written only what my mind dictates to me, and I have

---

[1]*gallabiyya*: the long robe, usually of cotton, worn traditionally in slightly varying styles by both women and men in Egypt, particularly in the rural areas. The *gallabiyyas* referred to here are heavy outer robes which women wear traditionally outside the home, although now European-style clothing has replaced the traditional garb to a large extent, particularly in the cities.

expressed only my own opinions in front of the groups of men and women students. In this instance, the lecture hall was filled with hundreds, or thousands, of them, and all were happy. The lecture ended with a profound and scientifically based discussion, and I returned home.

What followed that lecture, however, astounded me.

The Internal Security police summoned me and interrogated me. The Minister of Health had become angry. The Physicians' Syndicate had become angry. The publishing houses and the mass media were angry with me.

My name joined the government's blacklist.

When the authorities get angry with a writer, they can prevent that writer from publishing and can stifle the writer's voice so that it won't reach anyone. A writer cannot mount to the pinnacles of literature, and stay there, unless the authorities approve.

Everything in our country is in the hands of the state and under its direct or indirect control, by laws known or concealed, by tradition or by a long-established, deeply-rooted fear of the ruling authority. One day, I asked a leading literary man working at a major daily Cairene newspaper, *Al Ahram*, 'Why do you tell me one thing and write something else?' He replied, 'If they fire me at *Al Ahram* will you support my children and pay for their schooling?' Fearing servility, people became servile.

Most people here, even writers and philosophers, are civil servants.

It has been many years since I have read a great literary work, or heard of a single philosopher. I worked in the United Nations in order to free myself from the government, but I discovered that the apparatus of the United Nations is like that of the government, and the United Nations' experts fear for their monthly salaries just as all civil employees do. Moreover, the United Nations is led by men from the upper classes and the wealthy First World nations, while women from the Third World slide to the bottom of the heap.

The third knock on the door.

It must be the concierge, I thought, but I will not open the door for him. This concierge respects none of the residents of the building except its owner. He would never consider knocking on the landlord's door three times, or with this violence. People in Egypt have changed. The only ones who are respected any more are those who own blocks of flats or office buildings, dollars, open door firms,[1] farms producing Israeli chickens and Israeli eggs, or American chewing gum.

I resigned from the United Nations in the autumn of 1980 in order to end my self-exile and return to Egypt. However, my exile not only continued in Egypt – it grew. In government service,[2] my exile grew too. So I wrote my letter of resignation in the winter of 1981, stating that in Egypt everything foreign had taken on greater value than anything Egyptian, even human beings.

The fourth rapping, and the fifth, and the knocking on the door went on and on. This can't possibly be the concierge. However much he scorns tenants, his audacity wouldn't go this far.

I got up and went to the door. Long black shadows behind the glass pane, and the sound of heavy breathing. A shiver ran over my body. I was all alone in the flat. My husband had left before dawn for his village, near Tanta in the Delta to the north of Cairo. My daughter and son had gone out and would not return before night-time.

Thieves, perhaps. But thieves don't knock on doors.

Hesitant and apprehensive, I did not open the door. There's no security or peace of mind these days. I spoke up from behind the door in a voice which I made sure was loud and confident: 'Who's there?'

A strange voice answered: 'The police.'

The earth spun round for a moment, and I imagined that an accident had happened to my son or daughter, or my husband as he was on his way back from the village. But the voice was hostile; it did not give the impression that this was an accident report.

With shaking fingers, I opened the little opaque glass pane set in the door. My eyes widened in alarm: a large number of men armed with rifles and bayonets were out there, sharp eyes piercing the narrow iron bars, as a rough voice said in a tone of command:

[1] open door firms: joint-venture companies set up under the laws instituted by Sadat during his presidency (after the war of 1973) in order to encourage more foreign enterprise in the Egyptian economy.
[2] From 1966 to 1972 I worked as Director General of Public Health Education in the Ministry of Health.

'Open the door!'

A dream, perhaps? Reality mingling with imagination, the world of the conscious with the realm of the unconscious. My mind still did not believe that any of this was really happening.

'Who are you?'

'Open the door. That's an order!'

My imagination, no doubt about it. From childhood to this day, no one had ever spoken to me in such a tone of voice – neither my father nor my mother, nor anyone who had come into my life or knocked at my door.

Never in his life did my father give me a command. He discussed everything with me, even the existence of God. As for God, well, I engaged him in discussion, and God had to convince me of what he was saying.

Anger was gathering in my throat. 'What order?'

'The police!'

'You're not wearing police uniforms.'

From behind the armed band stepped an officer wearing a police helmet and a white jacket. On each shoulder, a bit of gold or brass glittered, and his white teeth gleamed in a polite smile.

'Please open the door.'

'Why?'

'We have an order to search your house.'

'I want to see this order before I open the door.'

'We don't have it with us at the moment.'

'Absolutely out of the question for me to open the door to you without seeing a warrant from the office of the Chief Prosecutor. That's the law.'

'You must open the door.'

'I won't open it until I see the warrant from the Prosecutor.'

I shut the pane. My whole body was shaking, and my heart was knocking violently beneath my ribs.

But the knocks on the door became more vehement. A nightmare, perhaps. I opened my eyes, trying to wake up, but I discovered that I was already awake and standing on my own two feet in the sitting room. The door was shaking under the violent knocking.

I managed to move my feet, forwards, backwards. I wandered

back and forth through the three rooms, not knowing what to do.

My home is a small flat suspended on the fifth floor between earth and sky. The street is about 20 metres below – if I were to jump out of the window my head would be smashed on the asphalt. No windows look out upon the neighbours, and the houses on the other side of the street are far away, while the cars below rush along at the speed of lightning. In front of the entrance to the building were a number of police vans, and armed men, rifles raised, rifle mouths gaping, looking as though they were turned in my direction.

What had happened? Had the world turned upside down, or had my small being been transformed into a dangerous gang which was threatening the world?

I raised my eyes skyward. The sky was in its usual place, and nothing under the sun had changed. But this was a world gone missing, half absent, indifferent, comprehending nothing of those severe knocks on my door.

Leaving the window, I noticed the telephone on my desk. I raised the receiver and dialled, but I heard no ring. I dialled another number; the phone rang on and on. A third line was constantly engaged.

The knocking becomes more violent. The walls are shaking, and I am trembling deep inside. A voice in my head tells me 'Open the door for them' while another voice, emerging from a remote place inside me, from a deep spot far back in my memory, in my childhood, insists, 'Don't open it! Don't give in!'

At every stage of my life I have obeyed only that voice coming from my deepest self.

I didn't open the door. I went into my room and put on street clothes: a white dress. I put on my shoes. I placed my identity card in a small handbag, with ten pounds, the keys to the flat and car, and a small white handkerchief. I began pacing around the flat. Here was my daughter's room: her bed and desk and bookcase, and a picture of her inside a small frame. Her tennis racket, a can of tennis balls, and sports shoes. I went into my son's room. There were his bed, desk, bookcase, his photo as a child, school notebooks and coloured pens. I went out into the sitting room – a large bookcase, music cassettes, and a black wooden head from Nairobi. I returned to my room: my bed, my husband's bed, the rows of books, his picture and mine together on top of the desk. The morning papers lay untouched on the small table. He had gone out early and had not read them. He is in the habit of reading the papers in the morning, whereas I leave them until evening. If I read them in the morning, the lies ruin my mood and I lose the tranquillity necessary for the novel.

My eyes were drawn by a large headline on page one: 'Precautionary detention measures against the instigators of the sectarian rift.' A few days before, I had read of the events of Zawiya al-Humra, a district of Cairo, where there had been a clash between Muslims and Christians in which several people had been killed. Egypt had never known sectarian strife. A hidden hand was playing with national unity. Were they doing in Egypt what they had done in Lebanon?

I heard the sound – like an explosion – of the door breaking. Their metallic boots pounded the floor in quick rhythm like army troops bursting forth in the direction of battle. They attacked the flat like savage locusts, their open mouths panting and their rifles pointed.

I could not see myself, but it seems that my appearance had changed, and so had my face and eyes. A devil must have been taking over my body . . . for I was no longer afraid. In the small sitting room, I stood before them, head held high, prepared to face them to death.

For a moment, they stood fixed, as if pinned to the ground before me. I must have appeared frightening to them, and I spoke in a voice which was also terrifying. 'You broke down the door. This is a crime.'

I don't know what happened then; perhaps my voice confirmed to them that I was a woman and not a devil. Maybe they were surprised that I was still in the flat and had not escaped.

They surrounded me, their breathing still heavy. Long, haggard faces damp with sweat. Open mouths panting. Noses curved like the beaks of predatory birds.

One band of them closed in, enveloping me like an iron chain, while another spread out in the three rooms. They searched through my drawers, and I saw one of them picking up the novel from my desk. I shouted furiously, 'That's a novel! Leave it alone, don't

7

touch it!'

But the man crammed it into a bag he was carrying. 'This is another crime!' I yelled in rage. 'How dare you snatch my novel from me? You have no business with it.'

Another man began leafing through the private diary lying on my desk, reading bits from it, his hands toying with the small clock which I keep there.

I heard their chief saying: 'Take her to the car, and we will catch up with you after we've finished searching the flat.'

'Search the flat in my absence?' I asked him. 'This is a third crime! If anything is lost, you are responsible.'

We descended the five floors. All the doors to the flats were shut tight. Bewildered eyes peered from behind the small apertures. We stood waiting on the ground floor. The rest of the men and their chief – the officer – were still inside my flat, scattering and going through my papers and private belongings. Anger was collecting in my throat like a lump. One of my neighbours came near, and they pushed him away quickly with their rifles.

The officer appeared, surrounded by his men, still panting and carrying my papers. The armed procession left the building. At a distance, people were stopping in the street, gazing at the awesome parade, their eyes full of fear. A woman carrying a child cried out angrily, 'Shame on you! Poking rifles in the face of a woman. Go fight Israel instead!' From a distance, a young girl waved to me, and I waved back.

In a flurry, the officer ordered the armed men to get into the vans. They clambered in, rifles on their shoulders. The officer led me to one of the vehicles and requested that I climb in to sit between him and the driver. I refused, saying 'I'll sit by the window.'

The officer looked at me in astonishment. For the first time, I took in his face: curly black hair, black eyes, a thick black moustache. Full lips parted to reveal very white teeth as he said, 'That's not permitted. It's against instructions.' His voice was harsh, but beneath the roughness I could detect a tone of weakness, and his eyes, despite their impenetrable gleaming blackness, held a note of passivity, a sort of submission to orders, or resignation to fate.

He tried to persuade me to sit between him and the driver, but I refused to sit between two men in this heavy heat. Two strange bodies oozing the sweat of hatred. It was absolutely necessary to impose my will from the start. I didn't know where they were taking me: to prison, or to my death? Nothing concerned me any longer except the issue of sitting where I wanted. Then let whatever would happen go ahead and happen.

The officer looked at me in the eye, and I fixed my gaze on his. I didn't blink, but he did, and looked at the ground. Perhaps he was thinking, and telling himself: even if my orders lack intelligence, I don't. There is no reason to stir up people in the street. Then, she's a woman and won't jump out of the door while the van is moving.

A look of despair came over his face. He got in ahead of me and seated himself next to the driver. I stepped up after him and sat next to the door.

The air moved as soon as the van was in motion. I took a deep breath. My will had won out. A simple matter, but as the first victory it was important.

People were still standing along the street. Some of the young men raised their hands and waved to me; I waved back. The officer jumped up in agitation on his seat, 'Please don't speak to anyone.'

'I'm not, I'm waving to them.'

The van sped off. My throat is parched, my heart is still throbbing, although heavily. My limbs feel cold, although my fingers still work normally. The leather handbag is still on my shoulder, and the shoes still on my feet. From the car window, an invigorating breeze reaches my face, and before my eyes are Giza Street and the zoo, University Street and the cars, people on the street, everything around me as it was before any of this happened.

But I am no longer the same. Something momentous has happened, and in the wink of an eye I no longer belong to the world outside the van, nor to those people walking in the street, nor to the ones in their cars going home.

Returning home seemed like an impossible feat, or like being transported from one world to another. I opened my eyes, closed them, and imagined that I would reopen them and find myself in my home, the nightmare over.

I opened my eyes and found myself sitting in a van, beside a police officer. Behind me, I could catch a glimpse of the tips of rifles jutting out from the roof of the van. I was still unable to believe this scene. The officer removed his hat and placed it on his knees, wiped the sweat from his face and head with a large white handkerchief. 'You really tired us out, doctor.'

My eyes widened. Was he addressing me? Was I still this 'doctor'? My memory began to return . . . I'd been sitting at my desk, writing the novel, and I heard the knock on the door, followed by more knocks before the door was smashed open with the noise of an explosion.

'Who tired out whom?' I asked in amazement. 'You broke down the door. That's a crime punishable by law.'

He smiled sarcastically. 'What law? Didn't you hear yesterday's speech?'

'What speech?'

'The speech given by the President of the Republic . . . Sadat.'

'I don't listen to speeches.'

'If you'd heard it, you'd know everything.'

'I'd know what?'

'You'd know why we came to you and where we are taking you.'

'Where are you taking me?'

'Nothing at all! Just a question or two, and you'll return to your home.'

'Interrogation!'

'No, no, simpler than that. Just a couple of questions, then you'll be home.'

If that officer had told me that he was taking me to gaol, perhaps the situation would have been bearable, or at least not quite so awful. At least I would have known where I was going. Knowledge, no matter what it reveals, is less painful than ignorance.

Ignorance is like death, or rather it really is death. If we were familiar with death then there would be neither death nor the fear of it.

Ignorance is fear. Nothing terrifies a person except ignorance. The amazing journey from the door of my home to the prison took several hours, during which I experienced the strangest ignorance in my life. It was exactly like being blind; it was as if they had bound a thick black covering around my eyes to shut out the light and the road so that I would not know where I was going. Each time I asked the officer where we were headed he replied with 'Never mind, its nothing at all. Just an hour and you'll go home.'

I followed the van's movements as it turned off the main road and entered a small side street. The light from the elevated street lamps was reflected in the tightly shut windows of the houses. A strange calmness this was. My eyes suddenly caught a light shining in one of the windows, but it remained shut. An old man, limping, entered one of the houses. A young couple strolled, hands intertwined, opposite a massive wall. The van lamps revealed their backs, and they disengaged their hands in haste, disappearing into the shadow of a tree. I imagined that the officer would jump out of the van and arrest them, but we went on, the officer looking ahead, absorbed in following the road, and saying to the driver from time to time, 'Right, left.' 'Left, right.' Finally, he said, 'Okay . . . here . . . stop.'

I didn't know precisely where I was. The officer and I entered a small building and climbed several floors. A short, stout, balding man demanded my personal identity card. He shifted his gaze from my picture on the card to my face and said, 'You wore us out, doctor. Why didn't you open the door for them?'

'They carried no written warrant from the Chief Prosecutor's office.' He looked at me in astonishment and I noticed that one of his eyes was smaller than the other. 'What warrant? Didn't you hear the speech?'

'What speech?'

'Yesterday's speech.'

'Are the Chief Prosecutor's warrants issued through speeches now? Or is it a question of speeches cancelling laws?'

He returned my card to me, and the officer accompanied me down to the ground floor. Behind the building, we descended a small staircase and the officer ushered me into a room on the lower floor, pointing to a small wooden seat in the middle of the room. 'Sit here for a bit, and I'll be back right away.'

I sat down, looking around me: an old man appeared at the door as if a crack in the earth had suddenly produced him. I saw him lift his hand as if in greeting, and I almost raised mine in response, but I realised that his salute was meant for the officer, who had already disappeared.

The man remained in place, standing by the door, coughing violently, his neck veins bulging. He wore a chain blackened with old sweat, and under the faint light of the single bulb his jacket had a yellowish hue. On his shoulder was something resembling a stripe, and his chest bore three brass buttons the colour of rust, one of which dangled precariously by a thread. The man rubbed his eyes on his jacket sleeve and I noticed a yellow rosary in his hand. On his feet were plastic slippers.

He remained standing, facing the door, his back to me. The sound of his breathing came to me monotonously, a continuous sound like that of air under pressure escaping from a hole in the neck of a closed bottle. He moved the rosary between his fingers. Allah . . . Allah . . . Allah.

It was not his voice, though, which had uttered the word 'Allah'; rather, the sound emerged from the movement of his chest, rising and falling with the motion of his hands. His finger joints cracked audibly. I swallowed a bit of dry, acrid spittle.

'Have you got some water here?'

He turned towards me. His face was full of wrinkles. His slightly bent figure scurried over to a shadowy corner and returned with a broken-necked clay water jug. Black marks, the shape of his lips, ringed his mouth, from which a putrid smell emanated. I hesitated after the jug was already in my hand and I had brought it near to my mouth. The man rebuked me vehemently: 'Drink it, that's water from the holy well of Zamzam in Mecca. By God, the finest people drink from my pitcher.' Taking it from my hand, he raised it to his mouth and the water gurgled down his throat. Wiping his lips, he hid the pitcher in the corner, then sat down on a wooden bench and began talking as if to himself. 'Every morning, I fill it from the tank in my house. I don't drink tap water these days. In the water pipes there's . . . I take refuge in God! These days, Our Lord is angry with folks. I used to put the pitcher in the window to cool it, but everyone going by in the street drank from it and there was never anything left for me. The world has changed – I never used to have to worry about the pitcher, or about water. I used to go up to the chief's bathroom on the first floor and do my washing for prayer. But the water started getting cut off even in the chief's bathroom. He's a good man, modest, not like the last one, God's curses on him. That one got a big promotion and was transferred from here to the Office of the Presidency. Praise be to God.'

Suddenly I heard a sound which I imagined to be a shriek of pain, a voice which rang sharply in my ear, though I could not tell whose it was: a young woman's? a young man's? a child's? My heart began to thud. I believed it to be the voice of my son or daughter. My rational mind told me that the van had carried me far from my house – more than ten kilometres – and I knew it was impossible for me to hear the voice of anyone at home, even if that voice was screaming. But I jumped to my feet, my heartbeat audible to my own ears, and the sweat on my body acting like liquid glue, plastering my dress to my skin. 'Do you think I'll be here long?' I asked the old man.

He stared at me with small red lashless eyes and turned back towards the door. 'Only God knows.'

'Is there no telephone here which I can use to call home? I want to reassure my family, tell them I'm here.'

I didn't know exactly what I meant by the word 'here', but the man gazed at me again, apparently in growing astonishment, before his lips parted in a smile which held a hint of sarcasm. 'A telephone! No telephone here.' He pressed his lips together quickly as if he had given away a secret when he wasn't meant to, and then he spoke again. 'I don't know anything here, I don't know if there is a telephone or not. These are all things which God alone knows. As long as you've come here, well, everything concerning you is known only to God.'

In the gloom, I brought my wrist close to peer at my watch, saying to the man: 'I was alone in the house when they came, and I'm sure my husband and children have returned and are looking for me. Besides, I don't even know why they arrested me, and why they leave me waiting like this with no one telling me where I'm going. They must be hiding something from me for some reason which they don't want me to know about.'

Stretching out his arm, revealing an old wound which he had bound with a bit of dirty gauze, the man said, 'They aren't hiding anything they know from you. They don't know anything, my girl, and they're waiting just like you are. Everyone is waiting, it's up to God, it's the order of Our Lord. What can a person do? Everyone has a specific mission. In the old days, the orders used to come in written form.'

My mind was wandering, but my ear caught the word 'written' and I'd already heard him say the phrase 'order of Our Lord'. In the voice of one asleep, I enquired, 'The order of Our Lord came written?' No sooner had I heard my voice ringing out in the empty room than I realised I was awake and remembered what had happened. 'I didn't open the door for them. They didn't have a written order, no warrant.'

The man shut his eyes and said, 'The order used to come to them written, but these days time is short and everything happens quickly, and the order comes as an urgent message by telegram. It is distributed to everyone in the form of an urgent telegram. It isn't written out by hand, or typed on a machine, and no one knows who sent the telegram except the Head Director. He doesn't know either, because he hears the voice over the telephone without knowing whose voice it is. He knows the tone of voice, though, and knows it's an order which has come from above, and that he is responsible for its immediate execution. The Director rings his bell right away and gathers together his officers. The officers here are good-hearted, and this officer who came with you is a very good man, from a good family. His father was brought up in the King's palace, and his uncle is now in the Presidential palace in Abdin. They are all solid folks, people with good family backgrounds, and if one of them tells you he doesn't know something, you can be sure he's telling the truth. He's not lying. He doesn't know anything and he is not meant to know, or else the secrets of the state would seep out. This is serious business which the Head Director is personally answerable for. Even I, small man as I am, I have to answer for everything too, whether it's big or small. Here, nothing is a small matter, and I'm meant to know the small things from the big ones, but the Head Director himself doesn't know such things. The world changes in a hurry, and the small thing becomes big without anyone knowing, or having anything said to him. Nobody tells me anything, they only give me these words, exactly: "Open the room and wait for instructions." I tell my wife that I have an emergency call. I might be away for a week, or it might be a month. She used to think that I had another wife, but marriage costs money, and I, praise be to God, have only enough to get by. I feed her and the six kids through honest work, and they are all in school, praise the Lord. I thank God and the government that education is free, but shoes . . . One pair costs my monthly wage now. O Lord, I say, seven pairs of shoes. And plastic sandals for me. Those slippers on my feet save the cost of a pair of shoes, and I have my old shoes, I save them for special occasions, or when I go up to meet the Director. But I have a boss with three stripes who isn't afraid of God himself. He told the Director that I wear the sandals during official work hours, and the Director called me in. I went up to him wearing shoes, and I saw him sitting there in shirtsleeves. He doesn't wear a jacket in summertime unless someone from the Minister's office comes over here. God inspired me, and I told him, "Your Honour, I only take off my shoes to do my ablutions and pray, and I pray five times a day, so I wash five times a day. And it's summertime – all that heat and sweat and, begging your pardon, I get wind because of digestive problems. I'm a poor man. I rely on God's mercy. I have seven – the children and their mother – to support." '

His voice was faint and remote as if coming from below the surface of the earth. Sitting on that small wooden stool, I could feel sharp pains in my back. I got up and began walking around the room. I stretched my arms and legs and shook my head and neck.

'Where did the officer go?' I asked him. 'Don't you know what's going to happen next?' Stretching and yawning, the man replied. 'Does any one of us know what will happen to him, let alone to anyone else? These things all happen by God's hand. As long as you've come here, don't wear yourself out thinking about tomorrow. You no longer have any control over your own situation – someone else does. You have to wait, we're all waiting. Who doesn't wait? Like you, I wait so I can go back to my wife and children, and I don't know when I'll be back and neither do they. Patience is a virtue, and whoever is patient achieves his goal. Listen to the words of an old man who has worked in this place for thirty years. There is no point in thinking. Leave your mind behind you and don't think about anything. As long as you've come here you should know that there are people who are doing your thinking for you, and the less you think about your own situation, the more quickly and easily the hours will pass. As long as you believe in God and the Prophet there is nothing to fear, because God never abandons his servants. Maybe you'll find it hard to believe that when I went up to see the Head Director that day, with shoes on my feet, he looked at my boss with the three stripes and told him I was wearing shoes. The chief said I was hiding the slippers, and I thought the Head Director would order a search of the room. He didn't though – he just laughed all of a sudden. I didn't know if I should laugh with him, for when he laughs I'm supposed to laugh too, even if there's nothing to laugh about. I said to him, "Your Honour, it's hot out there, and I take off my shoes because of the heat just as Your Honour takes off his jacket." The Head Director didn't get angry at me – he just went on laughing. He asked my boss, "Isn't there any mercy in your heart for this old man?" I swear by God Almighty that I've never in my life seen a kinder person than this Head Director, and I won't see anyone who has this much mercy in his heart ever again. He went on laughing, and I was laughing too and saying to myself, "There must be something funny about all of this." '

I heard the old man laughing, though it sounded more as if he were coughing, as he shook his head like someone choking on a lump in his throat. His eyes had filled with tears – it was either his laughter, or his coughing – and he wiped them away with a large, cracked palm. That hand went on concealing his face for a while, as if he had closed his eyes to sleep and had indeed slept, but then the palm came off his face, wet with either tears or heavy sweat.

The room was stifling, the air sluggish and absolutely still. An odour reminiscent of dust or the earth's depths pervaded the atmosphere. The sweat poured thickly over my face, neck and back, fine threads moving and crawling over my body like living creatures. I was still walking around the room, pacing back and forth like an animal imprisoned inside a cage. I stopped suddenly. 'I want to go to the toilet.' 'There's only one toilet here,' the man replied immediately, 'and it's on the first floor next to the Director's office. No one uses it except the two directors, or at least no one who isn't male. So what is a woman like you . . .'

Sudden anger came over me, like a tremor through my body, and I quivered sharply, looking perhaps like a slaughtered chicken jumping into the air. 'What do you mean when you say "a woman like me"? Do you think because I'm a woman I'm worth less than men? I'm a woman more worthy of respect than any man here, including your precious Head Director.'

The man's expression did not change. His faint voice sounded as if it were emerging from a grave or a fresh corpse: 'No one comes here except respectable people. Those who aren't respectable don't come to me – they go to another room, in the other building, and they are guarded by someone of a lower rank. He's the same one who sweeps and dusts the room, and he doesn't wear a uniform like I do. The guard here is respectable, because all the people who come here are respectable. Ministers have come here, and more than Ministers. They are all respectable folks and they treat me with respect. They call me "Mister". As for that other place, anybody who's there is not a respectable person. A hundred people or more stay overnight in the same room, some of them wet themselves in their sleep or as they're sitting there, and it's the guard who cleans the place. As for this place, it's a blessing. You've got a blessing here. Don't deny the blesings of God, now, say "Praise be to God." And smile, stop that frowning. Anyone who comes here and frowns is asking for trouble. They don't like people who get angry, or show joy, so don't do either one, just accept everything calmly without smiling or getting angry or sad. Sadness irritates them too, because they imagine that people become unhappy because they despise them. Not true, because the people who come here don't hate them, all the people who come here are respectable and don't know what hatred or malice is, and their hearts hold only love and belief in God.'

The man stopped speaking abruptly, breaking off as if he had died suddenly. I lifted my eyes to him. I had sat down again, and my head had fallen on top of my chest – perhaps I had dozed off. The man stood motionless for a moment like a statue, then clapped his feet together, raised his arm and touched his hand to his head. He continued to stand in the same fashion. I didn't know what had happened, but I saw a new officer entering the room.

'Let's go.'

'Where?'

'Never mind, nothing at all, just an hour or two and you'll go home.'

I don't know how I managed to believe him when he told me I'd return home after an hour or two. I thought he couldn't lie. His features did not give the impression that he was lying, or so it seemed to me. I hadn't really woken up yet from my little nap in the stifling room in the depths of the earth. The voice of the old man was still sounding in my ears like the voices of devils or angels reckoning the dead in their tombs, the wrinkles filling his face like that of my grandmother when she used to tell us stories, as children, about the tortures of the grave.

I went out of the door. A strong current of air slapped me, pushing me forcefully in front of the officer, so that I could see the van waiting. I really thought that he would take me home after an hour or two, and that after closing my eyes, I'd open them and see my home, husband, daughter, and son.

I was staring the officer full in the face at that moment. He was smiling, while his face bore that identifiable look of embarrassment or slight shame. His eyes held an odd expression of human kindness, not suggesting at all that he was a policeman, or a liar, or a stranger to me. It was as if I had seen him before, and his features were familiar. He asked me, as the van was moving off, 'Shall I buy you a Coke? You must be thirsty.' I almost laughed out loud, like a child, as I said, 'I'm dying of thirst.'

He stopped the van and sent the driver to buy the Coke. I had noticed that this was not the same driver, but through the small window behind my back I espied a number of armed men riding with us. The driver returned, carrying two bottles of Coke and two rolls, each stuffed with a piece of hard cheese. I wasn't hungry, but the officer jammed the loaf into my handbag, saying, 'You'll be hungry later.' His words filled me with suspicion and doubt, and my heart grew heavy with unfocused feelings – I was going to a place in which I would get hungry. But I threw off my misgivings and imagined that the officer's features were truthful and innocent. I did not understand that I was sketching features on to him, and that my hope of returning home had blinded me, making me incapable of seeing that the vehicle was heading a different way.

Exactly like a blind person, I hadn't seen that the entire city of Cairo had receded behind me, and that the street along which we were moving was not ours. I thought it looked like our street, and from a distance, looking out of a window, I saw a face resembling that of my son. I was on the point of shouting out to him but I closed my lips mutely.

My eyes wide open now to take all of this in, I saw that we had indeed left Cairo, that we were outside the city, and the van was turning off into a road which cut through cropped areas. On my right I could see vast fields stretching away in the gloom. To my left, the officer was sitting, and beyond him was the driver. Through the driver's window I could see the Nile waters gleaming under the light of the streetlamps.

I looked at the officer's face. I was not surprised to observe his police-like features, as if I'd seen them all along, and as if I had known since the start that he was lying to me: I would not return home, no, and the face of my son had grown far away from me, more distant than those stars shining in the sky. I lowered my head and gazed at my fingers, touched my right hand with my left. I am alert, awake, and still alive. I raised my head, and looked out of the window – an evening breeze, carrying the aroma of vegetation, the wind hitting my face with quick, light taps. The night wind was cloaked in the odour of autumn. I recognised the road, remembering my first trip to the Barrages. I had been a child in elementary school – I still had a photograph of myself, from years before, lying on the green undergrowth surrounded by the other girls in my class, with the Barrages in the background. The fields stretched away . . . in the distance I could make out a small house, with a light in the window, which resembled our house in the middle of the fields, the one we lived in when I was a child. The face of my mother loomed out at me from the darkness. My father's face . . . both had died more than twenty years before. In the darkness, their eyes glistened. Maybe it was a smile, maybe tears. My eyes were dry, my throat was parched. I swallowed: bitter saliva.

The van came to a halt suddenly in the open space. The blood froze in my veins.

A gang of armed robbers. They'll murder me and hide my corpse in the fields. Rape, maybe, before the murder.

Fears and old stories from the days of childhood came back to me. I prepared to defend myself, but I heard the driver speak. 'The van has stalled.' Everyone got out; the armed men enveloped me.

The driver opened the bonnet and he and the officer became totally involved in its repair. The sound of the motor came like rattling in the throat of a dying animal, and the van moved on its wheels in short, sharp jumps like a chicken under the knife. The officer withdrew his head from the bonnet and shouted at the armed men in an angry voice: 'Why are you surrounding the doctor like that? Come here!'

I began to stroll along the road. The evening breeze was mournful and calm. The fields extended before me in the darkness. I put a bit of distance between myself and the vehicle, walking fast. My heartbeat quickened with a sudden hope of freedom. Lucky for me that I was born in an underdeveloped country where the police cars are ancient and liable to break down.

For the first time, I could understand the benefits of underdevelopment.

The armed men had put their rifles on the ground and were pushing the van from behind. Inside, the driver was trying to bring the dead motor to life. The officer was swiping at his seat with a white handkerchief and cursing the driver.

I took a deep breath, and swung my arms and legs in the air. I began to walk forward without a single glance behind.

But I heard the sound of the van roaring, as its wheels ran along the asphalt. My fleeting hope vanished. These ancient vehicles are like cats with nine lives.

Once again, I found myself sitting next to the officer. Cap on his knees, he was wiping the sweat off with a handkerchief and his fingers were stained with black.

'Praise be to God,' he said.

'Who is alone to be praised in adversity,' I said. He laughed, but I didn't. My head was outside the window, my eyes wandering and my mind still resisting what was happening, not understanding exactly where this unknown trip with strange armed men would end.

I heard the officer speak in an abrupt tone of voice. 'Do you know that I've read your books and novels?' My eyes widened in amazement. Was he talking to me? Had I written books or novels? It was as if I had forgotten who I was.

'My books?' I enquired. 'My novels?'

'Yes, your books and novels.'

I took note of the police cap on his knees and I became totally alert, remembering what had taken place.

'That's incredible,' I said.

'What is?'

'I thought policemen didn't read books or novels.'

'We're like all human beings, and our profession is just like that of every man.'

The professions of men. 'Aren't there any women in the police force?'

'No, none in the police, nor in the army, nor among the judges or legal guardians or religious officials. These are all areas closed to women. You said so in one of your books, didn't you?'

'That's right.'

'We are an Islamic nation. According to Islam, women are lacking in mental power and faith. Or, are you against Islam?'

'There is more than one Islam. Every state interprets Islam as it wishes. Isn't that so?'

It seemed to me, as we talked, that I was carrying on an ordinary conversation with a colleague, during an outing by car along the banks of the Nile. But I caught sight of the glass pane behind us, the heads of the men and the tips of their rifles. I shut my lips tightly and remained silent for a moment, then asked angrily, 'Where are we going?' He did not speak, gazing at the road ahead of us. Presently, he said, 'You'll find out now. Don't rush things.'

'This is the Barrages road and you're taking me to the Barrages Prison. Why didn't you say so from the beginning?'

'Never . . . we won't take you to the Barrages Prison.'

I followed the road with my eyes. If not the prison, then what? Prison would be preferable; at least it would be a known quantity. As for this unknown destination . . . My eyes darted around in the darkness. The fields were still to my right, the Nile on my left. Under the headlamps, the Nile waters looked mournful, dejected. In a black sky, stars were shining; like ghosts, the trees moved soundlessly. The noise of the motor was especially loud over the silence and I could hear the wheels hitting the asphalt. The officer closed his eyes and drifted off to sleep. As the driver's eyelids drooped too, the van drove on alone . . . swerved . . . we would have toppled into the river if it hadn't been for a sudden movement of the driver's hand. The van jerked and the officer's head bumped against my shoulder. He opened his eyes, startled, and shouted at the driver: 'Are you asleep, you donkey? Do you want to kill us all, drown us in the Nile? Not enough for you, taking out a car fit only for sale in the flea market?'

The words shot from his mouth like bombs mixed with foaming spittle. He pressed his lips shut and stared straight ahead at the road, his eyelids dropping a little until they were entirely closed. His head fell to his chest and the rhythm of his regular breathing got louder.

The driver's cracked brown fingers clutched the steering wheel as if it were a hoe, moving it from right to left like a *shadouf*.[1] His lean, dark face was mottled with white: a sign of skin disease known in medical terminology as pellagra which results from malnutrition, and especially from a deficiency of Vitamin B. Pellagra weakens the muscles, numbs the nerves, and kills brain cells, afflicting the victim with a general dullness of the senses. This disease is widespread among the families of poor peasants in Egypt – as one can observe in those long queues of brown faces blotched with white. Years ago, I worked as a doctor in the countryside, and the driver's face reminded me of the faces of sick peasants. The officer cursed the driver's father and grandfather; the driver remained mute, head bowed, sad with the grief of thousands of years.

The van straightened out on the road, the sound of the motor monotonously regular and the officer's snoring audible over it. His lips hung loosely – thick lips, the lower one drooping over a full, square beard. His tunic, open at the neck, revealed a thick, pale neck, as his head bobbed and then fell on to a burly chest. Fine threads of white saliva ran down his lips, falling on to a bit of gold glinting on his chest.

I raised my head, looking towards the road. The lights of the Barrages were reflected on the surface of the Nile, but they were still distant as the car turned off on to a road so dark and narrow that it looked like a subterranean passage. We turned off on to

[1] *shadouf*: the dipper and lever by which the Egyptian peasant has raised water from the Nile to the fields for centuries.

another road, still darker and narrower. The smell of the crops and the Nile disappeared. The odour of dirt filled my nose.

At the end of the gloomy vault I saw a long horizontal pole blocking the road. The car stopped before it. The officer opened his eyes suddenly in alarm and wiped his mouth off on his palm. From the roadside, a thin man appeared, his eyes gleaming and darting about like those of a highwayman. He scrutinised the officer and vehicle for a moment, then his hunched figure hurried over and pulled the pole with a rope, or perhaps it was a chain, so that it swung high enough into the air to let the van pass. It fell into place once again, and the road was blocked behind us.

The van moves at a crawl through a long dark passageway. The air is sluggish, and the darkness is getting heavier; it's as silent as a grave in this place. The walls are as high as the Cairo Citadel. The sky and the stars have vanished. The van came to a complete stop.

My eyes collided with a huge black door like the doors of forts and castles from the Mamluk era. Several armed men approached us, images of the angels who toss dead souls into hell straight from the Courts of Inquisition. Their long and sharply pointed rifles and bayonets reminded me of the needles which used to be plunged into the bodies of witches in search of the mark of the devil. Their eyes were like bits of glass, and I was surrounded by eyes gazing at me, front and back, head to foot.

One of them tapped at the huge door with his rifle butt. A bald head and two shifting, glassy eyes peered from the narrow aperture in the door. He raised his hand in greeting when he noticed the officer and bowed.

The gap in the door was the size of a dwarf, and the threshold was high. I raised my foot to step up. I am tall, and I couldn't enter without bending. I doubled over: a body entering the mouth of a grave, my white dress the colour of the shroud. The officer's hands helped me to enter like the undertaker's hands would. It was as if I had seen this scene before, but when? Thick darkness, the odour of dust and rot.

I exerted pressure on my eyelids to open them, but they were already open. I saw a dark passage ending in a black shape, head wrapped in a white kerchief. Above the head was an electric light, like a single, open, red eye. The shape raised its hand in greeting.

Its rifle butt hit the cement floor, and one metallic heel struck against the other.

A hole opened in the wall; the earth swallowed me.

But not just as I had imagined. Once inside the prison, I was less afraid than I'd been outside it. Perhaps I'd expected something worse than what I saw, or perhaps one only senses danger when outside it. Once at its core, one becomes a part of the dangerous situation and no longer feels it.

Or perhaps it was the gentle smile with which the prison administrator greeted me. It was the gentlest smile I'd ever seen on anyone, man or woman, at any stage in my life.

I don't remember seeing this sort of smile on anyone's face. Could it have been a genuine smile? Or was I sketching on the features I wanted to see, just as I had done with the police officer? Or do policemen have this ability to smile as they lead one to the noose? The nearer the noose gets to the neck, the gentler becomes the smile, and the sweeter the voice, as they ask: What would you like? What will you have to drink? Would you like a cigarette?

'What will you have to drink?' I heard the official asking politely. As I was staring at this face, I felt a tremor run through my body. He was sitting at his desk, directly beneath an enlarged portrait of Sadat in military uniform with a baton in his hand.

The police officer was still standing there, holding a piece of paper which he extended towards the prison official, saying 'Please sign this – it says that you've received the detainee.'

The expression 'detainee' resounded strangely in my ears. I looked around me as if searching for someone else, then I realised that they were talking about me. I no longer had my first or last name, or my own personality. I became 'Detainee No.1536.' On the long list, my name was replaced with this number. The official signed for receipt of the detainee from the officer, and the officer signed in the prison register that he had delivered the detainee to the official. All this went on while I sat there, unmoving.

Then, with delicate fingers, even gentler than his smile, the official took my handbag from me. He emptied its contents out on to his desk: my personal identity card, my small diary, my pen, keys to the house and car, a white handkerchief, ten pounds and the roll. He shook the bag a few times, inserted his fingers into the inside pockets, and when he removed his hand it was grasping a small mirror.

He replaced the white handkerchief and the roll in the handbag and handed it back to me saying, 'The rest of these things are not permitted. We will keep them in the prison safe for you until you leave, God permitting.'

'Until you leave.' The words rang out strangely. Leaving here was like moving from death to life – transformation from one body to another, from one shape to another.

I noticed my small mirror on the desk. I stretched out my hand towards it, and almost had it in front of my face but the official's hand was quicker.

'The mirror is not allowed.'

'Why not?'

'It is considered a sharp implement, and all sharp implements are forbidden.'

Sharp implements? I am on my way to a place this dangerous? My eyes roved, over the walls, the ceiling: an ordinary office, just like any government office, complete with the face inside the picture frame revealing its teeth and tight jaws, over the head of the bald official, who had only a few hairs sticking out above his ears, and a gold or brass piece on each shoulder, writing something in the register. He raised his head, his eyes looking exhausted and red as if suddenly aroused from sleep. He pressed a bell and a woman entered: short, dark, wearing a greyish overcoat, carrying a metal chain on which were a number of huge keys.

His lips parted in a weak, despondent smile. 'Sorry, doctor. I would have liked to see you elsewhere.' He got to his feet and so did I; I was the taller one. He walked towards the door and stopped. On the wall over his head was hung a mirror in which I caught a glimpse of my face: just as it had always been, though pale and elongated, my cheeks and front teeth appearing more prominent than usual. My eyes were glazed with a light red but their blackness was just as black as it had always been – a shining blackness. My heart thumped with a sudden joy. I had been thinking I had died, or that my appearance was no longer the same. I noticed a black telephone sitting on a raised table, and I stretched out my hand, ready to dial my home number and reassure my husband and children that I was still all right. But, again, the official's hand was quicker: 'That's against the rules. Sorry, doctor.'

I gazed at the telephone as I was turning to leave, as if I was casting my final look on the last object in a world to which I would not return.

Then I raised my face. I was standing at the threshold. The woman was facing me. Her head was bound in a white scarf, her skin very dark, her face full of little pockmarks like the ancient ruins of a wall. White spots marked her nose and cheeks.

She walked ahead of me, her plastic sandals striking against the ground, the keys in her hand jangling, and the small round links of the iron chain looking like the links of a dog leash.

Part II
Prison

If the most difficult moment in the life of one sentenced to execution comes just before the guillotine falls on his neck, then the hardest moment I'd ever known came just before I entered the cell.

My eyes follow the movement of the chain clutched in the cracked fingers of a blotchy brown hand, around which the massive keys swing. The one key resembles a huge mallet with the head of a hammer and a long steel arm indented by jagged teeth.

In the dark, the shadows of the steel-barred doors are reflected on the high walls like legendary phantoms. Steel clanging against steel, the sound colliding with the walls and the echo reverberating over the inner walls, as if hundreds of steel doors are being closed and locked. A whistle as sharp as utter silence, and voices resounding like a whistle, like a waft of trapped smoke escaping through a narrow aperture.

The plastic sandals on the two cracked brown feet strike the ground. Her back is stooped inside a greyish overcoat, its collar blackened with old sweat. On one shoulder, raised higher than the other, a black stripe perches like a black feather on the head of a mythical bird or legendary beast of ancient times. The keys in her hand, though, give her more the appearance of a gang leader whose band haunts the forests or deserted wilds.

The gloom is growing heavier, pressing on my eyelids with a new density. The air, becoming sluggish, takes on a piercing odour which burns through the mucous of my nose like suffocating gas.

Her back to me, the woman stopped before one of the enormous steel-barred doors and inserted the key. Her breathing is audible, as if she were panting.

Her voice rang out in the darkness, remote, as if it were coming to me from beneath the earth or from an era long past.

'Go on in.'

She pushed open the heavy steel door with difficulty, budging it just enough so that my body could pass through. Her cracked fingers stood out against my white dress as she helped me to enter.

I've witnessed this scene before, long ago: now I remember. The dark cracked fingers encircling my mother's body, encased in its white shroud, and pushing it slowly into the open hole in the ground. Around me, my father and family stand in mourning garb, their eyes glistening with tears. My eyes are open and tearless, as my head collides with the steel of the door.

'Careful.'

Her voice, too, is familiar. She is still standing at the threshold; her eyes dilate with a fleeting light before disappearing.

The key turned in the door three times and the silence, like a single continuous scream, invaded my ear just as the sharp whistling had done. I blocked my ears with my fingers and placed the white handkerchief over my nose. On the ceiling was an electric light staring like a strangled, bulging eye. Metal bunk beds. Bodies moving inside black cloaks. Heads wrapped in white or black; the *higaab,* which shields the head and neck, covering the wearer's hair completely. Faces concealed beneath *niqaabs* – all-enveloping face-veils with small holes through which I could perceive the steady gaze of human eyes.

Had I fallen to the bottom of a well? Or sprung on to another planet? Or returned to the age of slaves and harems? Or was this a dream? Was I asleep?

No, I'm not sleeping. I'm awake, standing up, totally conscious that I am inside prison. This is the cell. Four walls and the steel-barred door.

I closed and reopened my eyes. The ghostly shapes were still before me. I could make out one of the faces under the yellow light, and I called out in delight.

'Safinaz!'

We hugged each other. She was a journalist and writer whom I hadn't seen for many years, and she had greatly changed. She hadn't been wearing a *higaab* then.

A pair of eyes were gazing at me through two holes in a black *niqaab*. 'Who is our new colleague?'

'Dr Nawal el Sa'adawi,' answered Safinaz. 'Author of dangerous books full of heresy.'

I saw a body moving on an upper bunk; she rose suddenly from her sleep and called out 'Greetings, Nawal.'

It was Dr Amina Rashid, a professor at Cairo University. Having met her a number of times in gatherings at my house and in the homes of friends, we had become friends. Happy to see Amina, I embraced her as Safinaz asked, 'Have you read the books Nawal has published?'

'Of course I've read them,' Amina replied, 'and my women students at the university have, too. They asked me to invite Nawal to the College so they could talk with her. These are important books which many people admire and like.'

'They're the books of an unbeliever and an atheist,' Safinaz responded.

'Have you read them?' Amina wanted to know.

'I read only the Book of God.'

'How can you judge books which you haven't read?'

A moment of silence passed. Some of the young women in *niqaabs* began probing me with questions about these books. Two eyeholes approached me and I heard a voice asking 'Do you pray? Do you fast during Ramadan? Isn't a woman's face a blemish upon her, a shameful private part to be covered?'

'The shameful blemishes are oppression, falsehood, and the eradication of the human mind, whether a woman's or a man's,' I said. 'The blemish is our presence in this prison when we haven't committed any crimes, and no investigation has been undertaken.'

The eyes inside the holes widened and took on a shine. I turned towards Amina: 'When did you arrive?'

'Two days ago. An armed group came to my house. My son was with me, and I was busy with moving my furnishings to my new flat. I asked them to delay my arrest at least until my son's departure and completion of the removal, but they refused, and brought me to prison. We weren't in this cell at first, but in the hospital quarters, in the same room with Farida al-Naqqash and Shahinda Muqallid. I didn't feel like I was in gaol. We had newspapers, a radio, and our own food. The door was open all day long. But they transferred us to this place, and deprived us of everything. What happened to you, Nawal?'

'They knocked on the door, and I refused to open it for them, since they had no warrant from the Chief Prosecutor's office. They broke down the door and brought me here.'

Amina's eyes widened. 'Broke down the door?'

Suddenly we heard the key turning. The door to the cell opened and a woman entered. The door was locked behind her.

I could see her face in the yellowish light as she came towards us. 'Latifa!'

Dr Latifa al-Zayyat. I'd met her twenty years ago and our shared artistic and literary predilections had been the basis of a friendship. Delighted, we hugged each other.

'I read my name in the evening paper, among the list of those who had been taken into custody,' Latifa said. 'When I got home, I found the policemen waiting. They were convinced that my sister was me.' She laughed and looked at me. 'Nawal, what about you? What happened to you?'

'I refused to open the door for them without a warrant from the Chief Prosecutor, so they broke in.'

'Things really have reached the limit for them to arrest an independent writer like Nawal,' Latifa commented. 'God have mercy upon democracy and freedom of opinion.'

It was nearly dawn.

'We really must sleep a bit so we can resume the struggle tomorrow,' I said, and we laughed. But the laughter came from heavy hearts, exhausted faces and anxious eyes. Amina returned to her top bunk, next to a Christian girl with a very young face named Nur. Latifa tried to get to sleep on half of a bunk, next to Safinaz, but after a bit she got up and placed her mattress on the ground. Wrapping a white headband around her eyes, she fell asleep.

I remained open-eyed, contemplating my surroundings: the scabby black ceiling, cracked walls, steel bars, a small window high in the wall, next to the ceiling, blocked with a steel grille. Women's and girls' bodies lying on the ground or on the black metal bunk beds.

I stretched out my arm and looked at my fingers, moved one hand

and grasped the other with it. Everything that had happened was real, not a dream. I was still wearing the white dress and the open-toed shoes which I had donned hurriedly as they were knocking at the door. My feet were slightly swollen – a sign of the long day's weariness. My throat was dry, and a ringing in my head accompanied a succession of filmstrip-like images. Events as old as childhood and new ones: the violent knocks, the noise of the door breaking, the yawning mouths of rifles, the shifting eyes of glass, the voice of the old man. The dark cramped vault, the horizontal pole rising and falling. The cleft in the great black door, the heavy, stifling atmosphere. I stretched out on the ground. Next to me was an iron bunk bed; on the bottom level lay a woman whose long hair covered her face entirely, and on the top bed was a woman wrapped in black from head to toe. Some of the other bodies extended full-length on the beds or the ground were half naked, while others were wholly swathed in black. I noticed an empty bed. Supporting myself with one hand on the ground, I raised myself, got to my feet, and walked towards the bed. No sooner did I sit down on it, however, than its fractured iron slats collapsed, so that I could see the ground below. I lifted the rubber mattress from the bed, placed it on the ground, and stretched out on top of it. Above my head was a black wall from which an unblinking electric light spilled red rays directly into my eyes, like a melting steel rapier, while ringing sounds, or perhaps a sharp whistling, poured into my ears like long strings of caustic liquid. Where were these sounds coming from?

I placed the white handkerchief over my face, blocked my ears with my fingers and closed my eyes. But the sounds continued to pierce my ears, and the light penetrated through my handkerchief and eyelids. Opening my eyes, I sensed a large space of burning pain between the eye and the lid which did not lessen, and a long stretch of time which would never come to an end.

Time is no longer time. Time and the wall have merged into one. The air is motionless. Nothing moves around me except the cockroaches and rats, as I lie on a thin rubber mattress which gives off the odour of old urine, my empty handbag placed under my head, still wearing the white dress and shoes in which I left the house.

I raised the handkerchief from my face and stuffed it into my ear.

Continuous ringing and sharp screaming, whose source I could not place. Weird voices and a commotion I'd not heard before. From where does all of this come? Do these sounds pass through the four walls, the ceiling, the earth's depths, to arrive here? Human and non-human voices alike. A sharp scream like that of a newborn child; wailing and moaning akin to the howling of wolves, quarrelling and cursing and a stifled sobbing. Raspy coughing, hands slapping and the sound of kicking. The whinnying murmur of water, what sounded like pleas of supplication, and chanting like the ritual of prayer. Frogs croaking, cats meowing and dogs barking, and over all a sharp whistling, the cockroaches' calls.

I was lying on my back in order to keep my head as far away as possible from the odour of the mattress beneath me. In the oppressive heat, I could feel the sticky sweat plastering my dress to my body. There was not a drop of breeze, and my chest seemed no longer able to move, either to rise or fall, to exhale or inhale. I imagined that I was dying, or that I had in fact died.

With the instinct of self-preservation, my eyes opened in alarm, as if of their own accord. I wasn't alarmed, or panicking in the true sense of the word, because I was sapped of all energy, in a state of fatigue and powerlessness near to death in which all reactions and feelings, including that of panic, were creeping away.

I don't know why I opened my eyes. I could have died with my eyes closed, but I discovered something I hadn't known before: a person dies with open eyes, as if wanting to see the process, or as if defending one's life with all senses.

In that instant it occurred to me that through my eyes I was sucking in the air which my chest had been unable to absorb. Perhaps this was the reason I didn't die. Although I could still feel and see, my chest failed to move.

And what did I see in that moment?

Above, I noticed a large yellow gecko clinging to the ceiling, creeping slowly along. A strange thought came to me: my gaze might draw him towards me, so that he would fall right on top of me. I closed my eyes, and then opened a single eye with extreme caution. I saw the gecko's legs moving before he fell suddenly.

If I had been in my normal state, I would have sprung up in fright before the gecko could fall on me. But I didn't budge. I felt the gecko running over my leg but I didn't move. Then I saw him jump off, startled, and disappear into a fissure in the wall.

My eyes widened in amazement, and suddenly incomprehensible feelings of happiness engulfed me. I closed my single eye in peace and slept until morning.

To this moment, I do not know how I slept, and I don't know the secret of that repose or the happiness which came over me all of a sudden – perhaps because it was the gecko which had taken fright of me rather than the other way around. Or perhaps it was the happiness of self-discovery, when there appears before one's eyes a new courage or self-confidence of which one was previously unaware, or when one disperses a fear or a phantom with which one has been living.

I had been living according to a bizarre illusion – or an irrational fear – of the gecko. My grandmother used to say that a gecko's touch would bring leprosy – in Arabic, the words for gecko, *burs,* and leprosy, *baras,* come from the same root word and sound nearly alike. I was a child when I heard this talk, and in my mind the *burs* came to be linked to the skin disease of *baras.* Even after I had studied medicine and knew that there was no relation between *burs* and *baras,* the linkage between gecko and leprosy remained strong in my psyche.

In prison, I learned what I had not learned in the College of Medicine. The gecko had crawled over my body and nothing had happened to me. Cockroaches had run over me and nothing had happened. I had lived with a fear of these small innocent beings that move with a marvellous grace in the night, searching for sustenance in the garbage and the wall cracks, and my fear now dispelled. I finally became capable of a deep and healing sleep as these creatures danced around me, causing me no harm.

The first night in prison I forgot, as I slept, what had taken place. I imagined that in the morning I would open my eyes to see my bedroom, my little white bed next to my husband's, the rows of books in the white bookcase, my son's face peering in from the door and my daughter's voice in the bathroom. I thought I would hear strains of music from the small sitting room. . . but I opened my eyes to find a high black wall full of cracks, creeping with black and white insects. Below me, a cement floor exuded dampness and rot, while shrieking voices which seemed to come from the depths of the earth, or at least from below the wall, were flinging out curses. 'Bitch, whore, daughter of a whore.' Oaths cast on women's sexual organs, oaths directed to all women's body parts. Curses of every sort, on mothers, fathers, grandparents, great grandparents. Damn the faith, damn the world. Weeping, sobbing, quarrelling, children's screams. The voice of a woman yelling 'Girl, call Fathiyya.' The sound of another replying at the top of her lungs: 'Which one? Fathiyya-the-Thief or Fathiyya-the-Murderess?' Voices shrieking and wailing. Buckets and tins clinking against one another. Metal colliding with metal and doors opening, shutting, slamming. Knocking across the walls, coming from below and above.

I shut my eyes. I reopened them. Where am I? I felt my head. What's beneath it? A cement floor. What's this unexpected odour, like the stench of a sewer? These black bodies, heads wrapped in blackness? Eyes peering through holes? I doubted that I was fully alert. But the cold truth crept over my body like paralysis. There I'd been, sitting at my desk and writing that novel, and suddenly they knocked on the door. I refused to open it for them. They broke in. The events came back to me in succession like a film tape running over rubber feeders.

For the first time in my life, I felt incapable of doing anything at all, as if I were before a force greater than myself. Feelings of impotence seeped into my body like a paralysis. I imagined that I could no longer move my limbs. I was so frightened by this thought that I found myself jumping to my feet.

I don't understand how I shifted from one extreme to another, simply because I discovered that my body could move as it had before. My sense of powerlessness was transformed into a feeling of power, and it was no longer important that before me was a wall and steel bars. The crucial thing was that my body could still move, that I could propel my feet along the ground, one after the other.

In the movement of my feet there was something akin to joy, like that of a paralytic who is healed suddenly and has started to walk.

I don't know the secret of the human faculty for adjustment and victory over the worst of circumstances. However, everything had become bearable, as long as my body could move. Perhaps I had begun with the idea of death or paralysis so that everything which followed would appear less grave. Perhaps this is the human being's capacity to adapt: beginning with the worst so that what is not quite as bad becomes utterly tolerable.

Less than 48 hours had passed before I saw Dr Awatif Abd al-Rahman coming into our cell. She, too, had been a friend for many years. I was happy to see her, and I embraced her, asking her with a laugh, 'What kept you, Awatif? Why so late?' She laughed as well. 'I was travelling; they arrested me at the airport. I came out of the plane and saw the police waiting. My son was there to meet me, and he walked with me as the police surrounded us. He didn't become alarmed or embarrassed, but walked beside me, proud of his mother. He had the newspapers, and I saw pictures of all of us. My son told me what had happened to you, Nawal, and said they'd broken into your home. Is that true, Nawal?'

We began to give our accounts of all that had taken place, as all our colleagues in the cell joined us. We were fourteen women, one still a girl – of different generations, ages, and outlooks on life.

From the moment I opened my eyes upon my first morning in prison, I understood from the motion of my body as I was rising and stretching the muscles of my neck and back, that I had made a firm decision: I would live in this place as I had lived in any other. It was a decision which appeared insane to me, for it would cancel out reality, logic, the walls and the steel doors.

Everywhere I had gone, wherever I had travelled, however far away the place, however unfamiliar, I would look around me in delighted wonder and concentration as if I had been born in that place and would die there, as if I had never known any other spot and never would. The faces around me, no matter how strange they might appear to me, seemed as if I had seen them before.

I found myself standing in front of the steel-barred door, jumping up and down on the tips of my toes and moving my arms and legs through the air, going through the physical exercises with which I had become accustomed to start every morning in my home or at the club. Between the steel bars I could see a piece of blue sky over the walls and wires, and I almost laughed out loud, like a child. Looking at the faces around me, I could smile and say, 'Good morning,' my voice ringing in my ears, merry and optimistic, announcing good news, resounding in the air around me as clearly as the ringing of pure silver – as if I were at home, as if these eyes around me were the eyes of my family.

To this day, I've never figured out the secret of the cheerfulness with which I greet any new morning. Does sleep wash the grief and pain from my mind? Or do I imagine with the naïvety of a child that the new day will bring something new? Or does my memory have an unusual capacity for rejecting sadness and pain? Sometimes I would accuse myself of naïvety or childishness, and I would wish to be free of these qualities. When my mother, and then my father, died, I tried to rid myself of this childlike demeanour, as I did when my daughter grew up to become a young woman, and when my son was no longer a child.

My mother used to scold me when I would laugh suddenly during a wake or funeral, while my father, too, would fix a sharp gaze on me and say, 'You're a big girl now.' Even my daughter said to me once, 'Mama, really, you're a grown up.'

Even in the midst of crises, in the hardest times and at moments which call for despair, this illogical optimism like that of an ingenuous child would spring from somewhere I could not fathom.

Sometimes matters would become even worse than they already were. Our circumstances inside the prison would sink to a new low, and we would hear news prophesying danger. Pessimism would darken the faces of all of the prisoners with me in the cell, and every one of us would feel surrounded by the most horrific dangers. We would sit together, silent, grave, pessimistic. Yet, something would move inside me suddenly, something built into me, the rebel, angry and revolting against this gravity, this submission to worry and grief. Rebelling against passivity and lack of movement, resisting defeat and pessimism, so that I would say: 'We will not die, or if we are to die we won't die silently, we won't go off in the night without a row, we must rage and rage, we must beat the ground and make it shudder. We won't die without a revolution!'

Then we would laugh – Awatif, Latifa, Amina and Safinaz. All of us would resist and laugh together, except for two, whose eyes knew no sparkle or optimism. One, named Boduur, was a young woman of about 30 who wore a *niqaab*. She would chant the Qur'an in tones which reminded me of Qur'an recitation at a funeral. I would think of mourning garb, and the black veils which female mourners wear wrapped around their heads, making them appear like the heads of crows as they stay carefully in single file, with their white handkerchiefs raised above red eyes or waving through the air around their black heads as they utter the harsh, sharp calls which convey the public expression of grief.

As a child, I made no distinction between the voices at funerals, mourning and wailing, and the ululating voices at weddings. I would laugh sometimes in funerals when the lips around me were all drawn tight, and I might hear someone saying to me 'For shame, that's wrong, *haraam*,[1] you mustn't do such things.'

In prison, the only word I heard from Boduur was *haraam*. Everything to her was *haraam*, taboo. Even physical exercise: a woman must not swing or shake her body. To Boduur, laughter was taboo because a verse in the Qur'an says 'God does not love those who are merry.' One time I saw her break into laughter without being aware of it; she raised her hand quickly to her mouth and stifled her laughing, murmuring 'O Lord, who hath all power to right wrongdoing. . .'

Her voice and gestures, and the black *higaab* which she wore, reminded me of my grandmother in the village, my father's mother – except that my grandmother left her face uncovered and knew nothing of the *niqaab* or the *higaab*. My grandmother was thin and agile, working all day in the field and returning to the house to cook and bake. But Boduur was plump and slow-moving, sitting all day long, hardly moving, and getting into discussions with her veiled colleagues concerning the contents of the Qur'an. Her 'discussions' were more akin to disputes.

The second one in our cell who refused to laugh was named Fawqiyya, and she was also a young woman of roughly 30. She resembled Boduur to a large extent in her features and movements, but she wore neither a *niqaab* nor a *higaab*. She was as uncovered as we were, but she placed a veil over her mind and could not imagine that there exist people who think in ways different from hers. Her discussions also took the form of quarrelling.

[1] *haraam* refers to a thought, word or deed which is considered to be against the law and practice of Islam.

Fawqiyya resembled Boduur in her blind faith in one idea, believing that anyone who did not believe as she did was an infidel, although her faith was not in God or the Prophet Muhammad as Boduur's was. Fawqiyya moved from her accustomed spot only rarely. She would remain sitting all day long, discussing politics, the party and the oppressed masses, and disagreeing with the others about the meaning of scientific socialism.

This was my first experience in prison, and I've always had an odd passion for 'firsts'. The first time I rode a donkey, as a child. The first time I went to school in the train. My first flight from Cairo to Aswan, and the first time I swam in the sea at Alexandria. The first time I lost my husband through divorce. The first time I lost my government job. My first experience of the pains of childbirth, those pains which would allow the head of my child to emerge from my body. The first time I placed a stethoscope to my ear and listened to a heart beating. The first time I saw the letters of my name printed in the press. The first step I took towards the first man in my life.

Every time I experienced a 'first', I would react by trembling. I would feel heightened joy and intensified fear, both, but the joy always overcame the fear. Even this time, as they were leading me to gaol, joy got the better of fear. How? I don't know. But deep inside of me I would sense a hidden secret which was wary of appearing before others, as if it were a sort of crime.

For I was born into a world which despises joyousness and those who are high-spirited. Even my mother used to fix her eyes on me in irritation or repugnance when she would see me dancing with joy. I used to think at first that she did not want me to dance, but I understood later that she did not want me to be happy. But why not?

When I had grown older, I understood that she, like me, was born into a world which has an aversion to merriment and considers all human pleasures to be perversions. The pleasure of discovery? Since knowledge is forbidden, this pleasure is taboo, for only the gods may possess knowledge. Ignorance is the blessing which God granted to his human servants, and whoever yearns for knowledge is like one who wishes to commit crimes and offences and longs for ill-gotten gains.

However, I was also born with a tempestuous and untameable impulse for knowledge. I want to know it all, everything, even death, and perhaps I have even been on the brink of death at times merely to satisfy childish curiosity.

As for prison, in my opinion it is like death in that it is worth discovering. All my life, I have regarded those entering and leaving prison as knowing something which I have not known, and living a life which I have not lived.

There is a difference, of course, between prison and death: it is possible for one to leave prison and return to a normal life, telling people what one has seen. As for death, no one returns or relates anything. Therefore, the experience of death has never lingered in my imagination. But how I had hoped to enter prison, on the condition that I would leave it in a sound state, and at the time I would wish! These are conditions which no one can guarantee, however. Prison remained in my imagination, like a nightmare, like death – the one who enters is lost forever, and the one who leaves is born anew.

In prison I came to know both extremes together. I experienced the height of grief and joy, the peaks of pain and pleasure, the greatest beauty and the most intense ugliness. At certain moments I imagined that I was living a new love story. In prison I found my heart opened to love – how I don't know – as if I were back in early adolescence. In prison, I remembered the way I had burst out laughing when a child, while the taste of tears from the harshest and hardest days of my life returned to my mouth.

In prison, I relived my entire childhood. At the sound of the spoon pouring sugar into a cup of tea, I would clap and dance with delight. The tea was like a mixture of black dirt and straw; the sugar consisted of brown bits over which ants crawled, but no sooner would I open my eyes in the morning and sniff the steam of tea from the pot than I would jump up from my spot. I'd pour the tea into a green plastic cup, and drink it slowly, sip by sip, its taste in my mouth sweeter than any tea I'd ever had, and all the faces around me beloved and near to my heart. Even those faces hidden under the black veils. . . when the *niqaabs* were lifted I could see faces that were shining, clear, overflowing with love, a cooperative spirit, and humanity.

Among the women and girls, I lived a communal life. I recaptured my happiness as a student at secondary school. Rejoicing, growing angry and fighting, mending our differences, feeling delight at the smallest things and growing sad for the simplest of reasons. Tears appearing in our eyes even as we smiled, and smiles breaking through while we still wept. From the disagreements among us in prison, one would have thought oceans separated one from another, and that each of us was an island unto herself. The dispute might grow yet more intense, but soon we would draw together, there would be harmony among us, and we would close ranks, a solid line facing the single power which had put us behind bars.

Nur was the only Christian among us. She had been arrested among the groups of Copts and other Christians they'd taken in. She was a girl of about 20, delicate and shy, who had no connection whatsoever with political work or the sectarian rift – for such were the accusations which were applied to anyone belonging to an oppositional group. We used to ask one another why, if the state was accusing those it was keeping in the prisons of instigating a sectarian rift and spreading hatred and malevolence among and between sectors of the populace, why, then, had they placed everyone together in a single cell? Why did they lock up the Muslim activist with the Christian, and 'the left' with 'the right'? Were the authorities hoping that some of us would destroy others, inside the prisons?

It was the complete opposite of this which happened, however. Within the group, harmony reigned. Inside the prisons, mutual understanding between all strands of the opposition was achieved.

Suddenly, a new order was issued: separation of Muslims from Christians, and the imprisonment of each group in isolated cells.

One morning, the head prison official in charge came in to our cell, calling out the name of the Christian girl, 'Nur.'

'Bring your clothes and come along with me.'

Her face went pale.

'Where are you taking her?' we asked in unison.

'We've had an order to separate Christians from Muslims.'

'Why? You can't lock her up alone far away from us!' We stood in closed ranks, to prevent her from being taken away, but he pulled her out by force. As she sobbed, we hugged her, one by one.

Solemnly, we sat down together without saying a word. In that silence we understood the truth of the matter. The latest imprisonment regulations had not been issued in fear of sectarian discord, but rather in dread of national unity.

The hardest part of any disaster to bear is its beginning, and the most momentous event in the life of a prisoner is the unexpected transferral from one life to another, from habits of a lifetime to new patterns which must be learnt. The hardship increases to the extent that the individual has been living a life of contented ease, or has been pampered, always expecting others to serve.

But I have become accustomed to serving myself. I work a lot and eat sparsely; I bathe in cold water in wintertime and have taken regular physical exercise since I was a child. I realised early that I needed two strong arms with which I could defend myself when necessary – in the street, or in a bus, whenever any man would try to turn my being into a female body which he could grab from behind or from the front.

While a student at the university, when my female colleagues were priding themselves on the softness of their hands, the smallness of their feet, the gentleness of their small bodies and the laxness of their weak muscles, I was proud of my tall stature and my strong, taut muscles. How had that happened? I don't know. I sensed within myself a rejection of the notion of weakness as 'feminine' or of femininity as weakness. I have never used powder on my face. However, I *was* used to washing my face every morning, brushing my teeth with toothpaste and doing my morning exercises, then exposing my body to the gushing water of the shower.

I opened my eyes that first morning in gaol and found no water in the tap, no toothbrush or toothpaste or soap or towel or shower. The toilet was a hole in the ground, minus door and flush, overflowing with sewage, water and cockroaches.

We began our life in prison by repairing the state of the toilet. That was the first point of agreement and it was the beginning of a common ground among all cellmates, veiled and bareheaded.

It is fortunate that the human digestive system does not

distinguish between right and left, or between one religious outlook and another. Whatever the difference in thought or politics between one individual and another, their need for the toilet is identical.

Our first meeting in the cell was attended by all the inmates. In fact, Boduur, who had refused at first to join even one session with those whom she labelled 'atheistic infidels', was the most enthusiastic of any of us about this meeting. I had not seen her so worked up even when praying or reading the Qur'an. I learned later that she was afraid to enter the toilet because of the cockroaches, and if it had not been for the intense constipation which was nearly killing her, she would have gone on like this forever.

Fawqiyya also was very enthusiastic about this first meeting. Like Boduur, she boycotted the toilet, not out of fear of the cockroaches but because she was unable to squat over that hole in the ground.

We all suffered this toilet problem together, and we all feared the cockroaches and insects, but for Boduur and Fawqiyya the problem was acute.

I thought at first that the constipation problem was the sole reason for Fawqiyya's enthusiasm about the meeting, but I came to understand subsequently that she loved to hold meetings, or rather she had become addicted to the practice of organising meetings. She had also become used to speaking in literary Arabic, articulating her words clearly and emphatically, and taking the chairperson's place.

In prison, chairs are one of the things which are prohibited. We used to sit on the ground. During the first few days it seemed that Fawqiyya missed chairs and speakers' platforms. After that, she created an imaginary daïs from a top bunk, to which she would ascend with great difficulty. After the bed fell as she was sitting on it, she would sit on the lower level, and finally became inured to sitting on the ground. But she never did get accustomed to crossing her legs or folding them beneath her while sitting. Like Boduur, she seemed to be against working her muscles, not because it was a taboo or because the Qur'an said something about it, but because of losing time in muscle movements for which she could see no obvious benefit or result. We used to laugh, asking her, 'Don't you believe in the use of any muscle in your body other than your tongue?'

In the first meeting, we began to distribute jobs and responsibilities among ourselves so we could achieve a human existence inside the cell. We took a collective decision to stand firmly together in facing the prison administration, in order to achieve fulfilment of the following demands:

1. Repair of the toilets and water taps; installation of a shower in one of the toilet enclosures so we could bathe.
2. Fumigation of cockroaches and insects, whether the sort that bite or not.
3. Obtaining bread from the market – *khubz mulki* – instead of the ordinary prison/military bread which is infested with worms and termites.
4. Closing up the gap in the wall between us and the mothers' cell to block out the voices which were irritating us day and night.

We had discovered that the strange voices, the shouting and wailing and howling and sobbing, were all coming from the cell of mothers imprisoned with their children who had been born in prison. Three hundred mothers, and three hundred children, inside one cell the size of ours, with nothing to separate us from them but half a wall – one which did not even reach the ceiling. If the mothers stopped quarrelling and shrieking then the children would start howling, and if the children ceased, the mothers began . . . and so forth, day and night.

If there exists a hell on earth it must be the mothers' cell at the Barrages Women's Prison. By comparison, our cell came to seem like the epitome of comfort and tranquillity, God's paradise on earth, and all the problems we faced were relative ones indeed. We were fourteen women in a cell, with a space of floor on which we could stretch out our bodies and extend our legs. At least we could walk between the beds.

Next door, however, with the same amount of space, were crammed hundreds of women, and hundreds of children – at least one child to every mother. The bodies of women pressed together, and clinging to children. . . insects biting the bodies of newborn infants. . . children screaming. . . mothers fighting for buckets of water, for bread, for a bit of sugar to dissolve in the water so the child could drink. . . one grasping the hair of another, fighting with hands and legs. . . cracked bare feet pressing on the bellies of children, their bare bottoms on the ground. . . eruptions of cursing, woman cursing woman, cursing her mother, her genitals, herself, the day her mother was born and the day her child was born, poor illiterate women, who had entered prison because of poverty or ignorance or oppression by men. Behind every one of these women prisoners is a man: a father branding his daughter for a life of thievery, a husband beating his wife into practising prostitution, a brother threatening his sister so she will smuggle hashish and hard drugs for him, the head of a gang stealing a young female child and training her to beg in the streets. . . the pits of society, the very lowest of the low. The tortured on earth. The other face of the system.

On the third night, holding my head, I felt I was going to lose my mind. They must have put us in this place so these voices would drive us mad!

Never in my life had I heard such voices – like millions of hammers striking blows over one's ears. And the voices, all of them, were transformed into a single, thick, scorching voice, almost a tangible one, like a cauterizing fluid.

Everything, everything else, had become tolerable. Termites in the broadbean paste, worms in the bread, cockroaches and bedbugs and lice and geckos and vipers. . . everything except that cauterizing liquid which spread through the ears and head, attacking every nook and cranny, and pressing on the brain like poisonous gas.

On the morning of the fourth day we were all standing together, veiled and bareheaded figures in a single row. Our first demand – before the toilet, before decent bread and clothes from home and going out into the courtyard for air and sun – our first demand was to block up that wall between us and the mothers' and children's cell with mudbricks and cement.

We were astounded when the prison administration hastened to fulfil this demand more quickly than any other: the next morning we saw men in blue tunics and the loose trousers known as *sirwals* approaching, carrying bricks, cement, and construction tools, and surrounded by soldiers armed with rifles.

No sooner had they appeared in the spacious courtyard than an unusual amount of commotion broke out in the prisoners' cells: frizzy heads peering out between bars, eyes sparkling, hands waving, smiles, laughter, winks. The entire prostitutes' cell went out to the courtyard to observe the procession of men. It was a sad march: young men who had lived for months, or years, inside the cells of the men's prison adjacent to ours. A dejected procession of bare feet, emaciated and pale faces, and defeated eyes. One of the men raised his eyes and saw the women and girls in white *gallabiyyas,* noticed their eyes sparkling and smiling. His eyes lit up suddenly, and he smiled before shifting his glance hurriedly to the ground. The others raised their heads and their eyes brightened. The young women drew near to the long, ordered queue; one stretched out her arm and shook hands with one of the men, and gave him a cigarette. He took it eagerly, as others stopped marching and began gazing at the girl, their eyes apprehensive. The orderly line of men became crooked and began to move in a confused mass, their eyes sparkling. The armed soldiers moved their rifles and the line fell back into order.

From between the bars, Boduur gazed at them from afar and let out a shout: 'Men approaching!' her *niqaab-*wearing mates leapt up; donning their cloaks, *higaabs* and *niqaabs,* they disappeared behind the beds and the walls. The *shawisha* – the prison official serving as our daily doorwoman and guard – opened the door of the small enclosure to the men, and then the door of the cell. They came in and finished constructing the wall between us and the mothers' cell.

The cauterizing liquid which had burned our ears was cut off. Unexpectedly, we felt that we had been transported from hell to a blessed spot. We exchanged glances of suspicion, and one called out: 'That's strange! Can we possibly believe that the prison administration is so anxious to make us comfortable that they're acting this promptly?' Fawqiyya's small eyes were raised towards the wall which had been completed, examining it in detail. Stressing her words, suggesting confidence and certainty, she said, 'I don't have the slightest doubt that the sole aim of building this wall was to install instruments inside it which will record everything going on here.'

Raised eyes wandered over the wall, and apprehensive glances went round. An atmosphere of silent despair reigned momentarily.

I laughed. 'This is excellent. Our views, which others fear to utter in front of them, will reach them quickly this way.'

Latifa laughed, and added, 'They will hear us laughing.' Everyone laughed except Boduur and Fawqiyya, whose facial muscles remained contracted. Boduur gazed at her veiled colleagues angrily. 'This loud laughter is taboo.' Fawqiyya's comment was voiced in a depressed tone. 'We've got to discuss this problem. Technology has advanced and they are rigging tiny taping devices everywhere, so what about the prisons, or the cells of political prisoners? They'll record every word we say and we won't be able to breathe without having electronic devices transmitting the movement of our chests and the shape of our breaths.'

The air was growing heavier. Our chests began to move with difficulty, if at all. I felt I was suffocating. Trying to lighten the atmosphere of despondency, I said, 'Let them record what they wish, and we will breathe exactly as we want, and say what we want, for we're in prison because we demand freedom and refuse to be bound. Are we going to put chains on ourselves inside prison? Are we going to strangle ourselves with our own hands? Anyway, what more can happen to us? The only thing lacking is death.'

'True,' said Latifa, 'All that's missing is death. What more is there after prison?' Awatif laughed. 'At least before we die they will hear our views.'

One of the *munaqqabas* – those who wear the *niqaab* – spoke in a fervent voice. 'By God's greatness, I'll say all I have to say and let them hear. Just let the tyrant hear!'

'Down with the detention order!' said another. 'And the Law of Shame, and the morals of the village!' The slogans came in quick succession. 'Down with the Law of Suspicion, and the Court of Values! Down with the Open Door Policy, and Camp David, and normalisation of relations! Down with dictatorship! Down with the new colonialism, imperialism, and Zionism! Down with "my friend Carter", and Reagan, and "my friend Begin"! Down with lies and forgeries!'

Everyone repeated the slogans in unison, and laughter pealed out through the cell. Someone winked in the direction of the new wall and said, 'Record, uncle, record.'

During the first few days, things were tense and strained. Alarm was widespread, within the prison and outside. On the radio blared Sadat's trumpeting voice without cease, while his picture was a constant presence in the newspapers and on the television screen – opening his mouth as wide as could be, showing his whole set of teeth, tightening his jawbone, as he gestured with his fist in the air.

'I will have no mercy. . . I will crush and eradicate them. . . I will have no mercy. . .'

On the television screen, he was surrounded by men of state, army people, Internal Security policemen, military intelligence officers, journalists and media people, members of the People's Assembly and the Consultative Assembly, the Socialist Prosecutor's apparatus, senior civil servants and top ministry officials, leading private sector businessmen, representatives from firms established under the Open Door policy and foreign banks and Green Revolution projects and food security projects, those who were to represent prosperity and the pillars of security and peace.

People were too afraid to walk in the streets. Whoever had a relative in prison became uneasy, anticipating a knock on the door and expecting to be taken to prison themselves. Raising a telephone receiver automatically brought the thought that one's voice would go directly to the Internal Security Police. Trying to fall asleep in one's bedroom, one would turn and gaze at the walls, imagining them to be crammed with taping devices and electronic lenses.

We were meant to know nothing of what was going on outside prison, or inside either. We were meant to remain inside the cell, behind the two steel doors, without newspapers, radio, letters, family visits, or food from home, banned from all communciation or conversation through the bars with any of the prisoners strolling in the outer courtyard.

No one came into our cell regularly except the *shawisha,* the female warden in charge, the male prison head, and officials representing the Ministry of the Interior or the Internal Security Police. Every day, we would see those officials in police garb or dark glasses, dispatched to our cell repeatedly in unannounced visits which surprised the prison administration as much as they did us. They all looked alike: similar features, facial muscles taut as if stretched on wires, identical gait and gestures, all carrying batons with tapered heads in their left hands, in their right clutching rosaries of small yellowish beads, which they fingered without cease, showing fingernails cut with great precision into pointed shapes ending with tips thin as needles.

Their faces were all cleanshaven, their hair cropped in short uniform fashion, as if they had all gone to the same barber. They all exuded the scent of aftershave cologne. This aroma would waft over the cell, striking us as peculiar. The *shawisha* would unlock the gate of the small enclosure for them, and then would let them into the cell, where they would fan out before us like young locusts still without wings – for the wings were hidden in the ample folds protruding over the belts of their trousers.

Their senior member or chief officer would precede them, in full police uniform, the stars shining on his chest and shoulders, waving the taper-headed baton in the air, the muscles of his neck and back visibly taut. His deputy moved by his side, also in police garb – fewer stars on his epaulets, though. Beside the deputy would be *his* aide, in official dress too, his face masked by dark glasses. The file continued: the aide's deputy beside him, then the more junior aide, shorter in stature and wearing dark glasses with smaller lenses, the protrusion of his stomach ove his belt less marked.

At the end of the row stood the prison physician, minus white coat, wearing a police uniform like the others, hastening his step in order to keep his ear to the mouth preceding him. Behind the physician would stand the female warden, standing erect next to the male prison head, resembling him but wearing civilian dress rather than a uniform. Her facial muscles and full lips were taut and compressed, her arms drawn tight over her ample chest and her stout calves held together tightly, quivering over high aluminium heels. The *shawisha*, by her side, would try similarly to tighten the muscles of her back, stooped inside her grey overcoat with the faded black stripe on the shoulder, her veiny brown hands compressed over her chest, her cracked feet inside those plastic sandals.

Some of us would be sitting on the floor, others on the beds, staring fixedly, our eyes wide open – whether bare or hidden behind a *higaab* or gazing from behind the holes in the *niqaab*. We would follow the movement of that long queue composed of the upper echelons of the state's police administration.

Their senior gave his head a shake as he swung the baton in his hand, thrust his shoulders upward, and studied the walls closely before turning his gaze to the faces before him.

'I hope you're comfortable here.'

My cellmates exchanged sardonic glances, and one gibed, 'Very comfortable . . . with your presence!'

A burst of laughter escaped from beneath a black *niqaab*. Ignoring it the prison head spoke again. 'Within the scope of the authority given to us, and within the limits of the instructions which have reached us thus far, we are doing our best to fulfil your requests. Isn't that right, Mr Abd al-Rahim?'

He glanced at one of the senior prison administrators, who answered him hastily. 'Yes indeed, sir. The wall has been built up, all the way to the ceiling, to keep them from hearing the voices of the mothers and children. A shower has been installed in one of the lavatory enclosures, and we have notified the Insects Division of the Ministry of Health to despatch a crew to exterminate the insects in the cell. Just for these women, we have assigned someone from the prostitutes' section to be on duty, to clean this ward regularly, and they've started getting bread from outside. We are prompt, your excellency, in answering their demands.'

One of the young women stood up. 'I want a piece of paper and a pen to write a letter to my mother, and –' 'No pen and paper' came the abrupt reply, interrupting her sentence. 'That · is utterly forbidden. Anything but pen and paper. Easier to give you a pistol than pen and paper.'

The comparison between a pistol and a pen and paper rang in my ears oddly, like a line from a farce. I thought I must be sitting in a theatre. I had not imagined that pen and paper could be more dangerous than pistols in the world of reality and fact.

However, this seemed to be the case – or the least of it. We had seen women prisoners undergoing body searches. If the female warden or *shawisha* happened to find a scrap of paper as she poked her fingers inside a woman's body, the gaol was turned upside down.

The prison head began strolling around the area, followed by the queue. He cast a glance over the toilet enclosures, then turned to us and remarked, 'You're in luxurious surroundings here. You have a toilet. We always look after a woman's comfort. We couldn't possibly treat women as we do the men.'

He turned to gaze at me. 'Isn't that right, Dr Nawal? Or do you want equal treatment with the men detained in Tura Prison?'

'I would have to see how those detained in Tura are living before I could offer my judgement.'

'This is a paradise compared to other prisons.'

'Then why don't you come and live in paradise?' asked Awatif.

His features contracted. 'Do you have any other requests?'

'We want clothes from home,' said one of the young women. 'I came here in this one dress which I have been wearing day and night. Whenever I wash it, I sit beside it until it is dry and then put it on again.'

The veiled women covered their eyes with their hands in mortification – it must have occurred to some of them that this row of men was envisioning the speaker sitting in the nude waiting for her dress to dry out. The young woman who had spoken, discomfited too, lowered her head.

'This is an issue which doesn't cause us any embarrassment,' I said, 'But it *is* embarrassing for the policemen who lied to us and did not explain that they were leading us to prison. I, too, wash out my single dress and wait until it dries.'

The prison head nodded. 'This matter is easily taken care of. Right, Shafiq Bey?' He looked at the top-ranking Internal Security official present, who nodded, jiggling the dark glasses which shielded his eyes.

'Of course, Salah Bey, sir, this is a very simple matter and the clothes will reach them in a few days.'

The taut lines in Salah's face disappeared suddenly and he was almost smiling as he said, 'Fine, fine. Then there is no problem.'

The smile was borne along as if by a fast-spreading contagion, from Salah Bey's lips to those of his deputy, then to his aide, and then the others, one after the other, until it reached the female warden and *shawisha*. The doctor was the last to smile, hesitating a moment to open his compressed lips. Perhaps he was trying to will his mouth to be completely independent of the prison head's, but it seems that he had second thoughts and remembered that he was a civil servant in the Ministry of the Interior, his situation no different from that of the female warden. His lips parted in a smile. In fact, he didn't stop there: he threw back his head and laughed out loud, confirming his existence and establishing his identity as independent of that of the warden or *shawisha*.

'How will we obtain clothes from home?' asked a *munaqqaba* in a barely audible voice. 'Will our families be permitted to visit us and bring clothes with them?'

The Internal Security official replied swiftly, 'No, visits are not allowed. Whoever needs clothes will write a request to that effect, listing the clothes she wants and submitting the request to the Internal Security policeman in charge.'

'Great, great,' Salah Bey called out. 'So there's no problem.' He turned towards the door to leave the cell, the queue following him, but I called out to him. 'Mr Salah. . .'

He turned in my direction, his eyes darkening in sudden anger, perhaps because I had addressed him by his first name or with the title 'Mr' instead of something more elevated like 'Bey'.

'There *is* a problem, Mr Salah.'

All the eyes darkened in faces now grown taut.

'The problem is that we do not know how to write these requests without having access to pens and paper.'

Muscles relaxing, the prison head nodded in agreement. 'You have a point.' The he looked at his aide, who looked at the Internal Security official, who looked at the Internal Security policeman who said, 'That's no problem. The lady warden will bring you a pen and some paper to write these requests.' Through his dark glasses, he fixed his gaze on her, repeating, 'To write these requests only. One piece of paper for each prisoner. She'll write her request in front of you and then you will take the pen and the request from her, immediately.'

'Just as you say, sir,' the warden sang out.

One of the veiled women stood up. 'I want to write a letter to my mother. They arrested me in the street, while she was at home with no idea of where I was. She must be wandering the streets looking for me.'

'Don't worry,' said Salah Bey. 'She must know by now.'

51

'Know what?'

'She knows you're in a safe place and there's nothing to fear,' said the Internal Security policeman. 'The President of the Republic announced that the Precautionary Detention Order means nothing other than protecting you in a secure place until the Socialist Prosecutor can begin the investigations.'

Laughter rang out through the cell.

'And when will the Socialist Prosecutor start the investigations?' asked a bareheaded woman. The Internal Security official raised his hands in a gesture of ignorance, saying 'God only knows. Like you, we know nothing. We just wait for instructions from above.'

A pair of small, ingenuous eyes gleaming from behind the eyeholes of a *niqaab* followed the movement of his hands and raised her eyes to the ceiling, then breathed out in astonishment, 'From above?'

Salah Bey replied at once, waving his baton in the air. 'We are all awaiting instructions from above. Hope for the best, God willing, for you live in a state which runs according to laws and institutions. Anyone whose innocence is established will not stay in prison.'

He turned to walk towards the door. My mind seemed numbed – until I got to my feet. Abruptly, all that had happened returned to my memory, as if I had been asleep and had awakened: the vehement knocks . . . the sound of the door breaking, like an explosion . . . the rifles levelled at my face . . . the voice of the old man . . . the long, dark road . . . the gloomy, obscured hours of journeying towards an unknown destination . . . the chain, keys, bars, insects . . . insomnia . . . my son and daughter and husband circling the streets, searching for me . . . the days and nights, part of one's lifetime going to waste in the darkness. After all of that, these men smelling of aftershave cologne come along, after they've had a full night's sleep, changed their clothes, bathed with soap, and had something to eat and drink. They come to display their police garb and gleaming stars, while we sit on the floor, our faces exhausted and pale, our eyes anxious and showing the effects of sleeplessness, our feet grimy, heels blackened from walking through the dusty enclosure then plunging them into the sewer water in the toilet. And they're telling us that we are in paradise and in a secure place, and that whoever's innocence is proved will get out!

'Hey, Mr Salah!' I called out in a loud voice.

He turned to me, and the entire queue turned with him. I saw their widened eyes staring at me, and I began staring back at them, sensing that my chest was going to explode in anger. However, I remembered that those figures were awaiting orders from above, that they do no more than execute orders. I got control of my rage and spoke in a voice which was empty of anger, but which still cut coldly like a sharp knife edge.

'What you said just now about this innocent woman who will leave prison after her innocence is proved, Mr Salah, is unintelligible to the mind or to logic. Can't you see that these words are contrary to the law? If this innocent woman were to leave prison after a month – or a year – then who, I wonder, would compensate her for those days and nights which she had spent here? How can you say this to us and then leave just like that, smiling, your conscience at rest? How can you say "Fine, fine, there are no problems then"? The first problem, Mr Salah, is that the innocent woman should never have been here in the first place. Secondly, here we are, we've been here for days, for weeks, and no one has begun any investigative procedures with us. Not one of us knows what the charges are against her. They invaded our homes by armed force, without warrants from the Chief Prosecutor, and to this day our families don't know anything about our circumstances, and we have no idea how they are. Among us are mothers who've left unweaned babies, and students who have been taken away from their studies, and workers who have been suspended from work or from their positions, and writers who have stopped writing. One of us is in her last weeks of pregnancy and she has had no medical care, while there are others who have contracted scabies infection. We are all threatened by the widespread diseases here, which are communicated by the flies and insects as well as by the air which carries smoke, dust and microbes of filth or tuberculosis. Can you possibly call this a safe place? And say that we are under a rule of law? Where is the law, and why hasn't the investigation started yet? How can we be imprisoned without an investigation?'

I was on my feet, muscles tense, eyes fixed on the face of the queue's chief, my back to my cellmates. I saw the faces before me, without exception, tighten into frowns, while the eyes darkened.

The atmosphere was becoming electric. But the queue was standing motionless and mute. Each individual was looking at the next out of the corner of an eye, and all the eyes were peering towards Salah Bey to see what he would do so that they could do likewise. Salah Bey was standing rooted to the spot, his face in my direction but his eyes raised skyward as if waiting for instructions to descend from on high – instructions which would tell him what to say in response to me.

I sensed a movement behind me. I noticed out of the corner of my eye that my cellmates had stood up together, heads and backs upright. The uncovered faces gave an impression of anger and those hidden under *niqaabs* were held threateningly rigid, while the eyes glinting through eyeholes were preparing for assault.

Salah Bey's upward gaze remained unchanged, and he was silent. Then his eyes descended with a movement which suggested disappointment. Perhaps no instructions had come down to him, and therefore it had become imperative for him to act on his own, or maybe contradictory thoughts were going round in his head and he didn't know whether or not to get angry. Truly, the affairs of politics are as crafty and unpredictable as a wicked imp. No one knows what may happen tomorrow, or even an hour from now. There are no longer any guarantees that anyone will retain his or her position. Any ruler, in the largest state, can vanish with the firing of a single bullet. Any government can disappear in the wink of an eye with a coup in the army, or a revolution among the people. Overnight, the government official finds himself in prison, while the one in prison is now in government, and praise be to the Everlasting in all cases. He bowed his head as if in thought.

'Where is the law and where is the state which runs by law,' asked Latifa hotly, 'when we are here in prison without having committed any crimes, and without any investigation? How can we be charged and imprisoned before we are tried? This is tyranny. . . and it's an abuse of human rights.'

Awatif's voice was rebellious, agitated. 'We should be tried first according to the law and then imprisoned, not the other way around. That's what the constitution says.'

'I don't know why I'm here,' remarked one of the *munaqqabas*. 'I was on my way to visit my aunt and they arrested me in the street.'

'If there are accusations against us,' added Amina, 'then why don't they carry out an investigation? Why are they postponing it? One hour in prison without having committed a crime is equal to ten years.'

He remained silent, listening, and no one had any idea what he would do. Then he nodded, smiled artificially and spoke in a completely calm voice. 'It wasn't I who put you in prison. I only carry out orders. So far no orders have reached me concerning the investigations. I am still waiting for instructions from above.'

The two naively innocent eyes peering from the holes in the *niqaab,* the eyes of a child of sixteen, knowing nothing of life – these eyes followed the movements of his hands as he raised them high. She called out in a childish voice, 'From on high? From where?'

The Internal Security official jerked his head upward, saying, 'From Our Lord.' Without warning, we saw Boduur flare up, lifting her hand in supplication. 'God Almighty grant us His forgiveness. His Exalted Being does not issue instructions about detention in prison. An idol has been erected, a false god! God take him!' 'Amen,' repeated all the veiled women in unison.

The *shawisha*'s lips parted automatically, and she, too, said, 'Amen.'

Salah Bey threw an angry gaze at her and said in a tone of command, 'Quiet, you, keep your mouth shut!'

'I didn't say anything,' responded the *shawisha* in a faint voice. 'I only said, "Amen".' Salah exploded. 'I said, "Quiet". Don't speak when I am present!'

All of his suppressed rage came pouring out on her head, for she was merely a *shawisha*, on the very bottom rung of the employment ladder. He could vent his anger on her without drawing a response. Indeed, the *shawisha* recoiled and shrank against the wall.

Salah Bey, to the contrary, raised his head, features smoothed out now as if his authority and prestige had been restored. He turned and left the cell for the enclosure, raising one foot so high that his shoulder jutted upwards, while the other jolted downwards, then planting that foot on the ground so that the lower shoulder moved skywards as the higher one dropped. His joints and extremities gave him the appearance of a marionette, wired tightly with strings from above the proscenium.

Behind him, every member of the long queue was trying to walk just as he did. At the rear came the *shawisha*, the keys in her hand. She went out behind them, locking the double steel doors.

The warden, Shukriyya, returned, accompanied by the *shawisha* carrying a wooden stool. The warden seated herself on the stool, and I could see a few pieces of white paper and a pen in her hand. She counted the paper, piece by piece, and then counted us, one by one.

'Fourteen women, and fourteen pieces of paper,' she said. 'You can each have one piece. Write down the clothes you want now, here before me, then give me your request and the pen.'

I have got into the habit of writing regularly. Writing slices time, slashing it swordlike into pieces. In prison time extends, on and on, as though it were timelessness.

I wrote only at night, however. During the day, the surveillance over us was heightened and reinforced. They would lock those two steel doors upon us so that we could only move inside the cell, or within the little dirt enclosure in front of the cell – a space surrounded by four high walls, crowned by barbed wire. We used to go out to this tiny courtyard and remain there from half past eight in the morning until four o'clock in the afternoon. I would take a few minutes to circle the enclosure fifty times, then I'd stand just behind the door gazing through the bars at the prisoners walking in the large courtyard, their uncut frizzy hair streaming and the rips in their long white *gallabiyyas* revealing large areas of flesh. Carrying buckets of water on their heads, these women walked with slow, heavy steps like a herd of diseased cattle being led to the slaughterhouse.

One of them, who was especially tall and slender, approached the bars of the door. I could see her sharply-protruding cheekbones, a smudge of mud on each cheek, wide eyes sunken in their sockets like two deep trenches, black irises prominent against the white of the eye: coals glowing with a black flame. . . a black tongue of fire leaping from the ashes before the final incineration, or just before the fire goes out completely.

From where I was standing, behind the bars, those fiery eyes pierced mine like a scorching tongue of flame which I could feel between my eyelid and my eye.

She grasped the bars of the door. Her fingernails were long and pointed; black mud filled the space between nail and flesh. Her hair was a long mass of tight curls. She looked like a cave-dwelling woman who has lived in the bowels of the earth for centuries, whose mind has caught fire with a mad flame which can find no exit but the two eye sockets in her skull.

She moaned in a voice like a drawn-out whistle. 'A loaf . . . give her a loaf of bread.'

I glanced around, enquiring, 'Her?'

Pointing a spiky fingernail at her own chest, she repeated, 'Give her a loaf of bread.'

She was referring to herself in the third person. She was suffering from schizophrenia, a condition in which one tries to heal crushing pain by imagining that it is happening to someone else.

There was no bread in our cell. It was still early morning, and *Shawisha* Nabawiyya had not come with our bread. At first, each of us had been given two loaves per day. We had lodged our protest with the prison administration, and soon we were getting three loaves apiece of bread from outside, the sort that is sold normally, rather than old bread or the regulation prison bread from government bakeries.

The first day, I hadn't eaten a single bit of my bread. When I opened up the pitta loaf, I was treated to the sight of white worms and black termites looking like pinheads stuck into the dough of the bread. On the dish of *ful* – broadbean mash – too, I saw more of those little black and white creatures than I could count, overflowing from the surface of the dish.

That plate of *ful*, and the loaf placed over it, had remained next to the wall all day and all night, until dawn. I opened my eyes to the sound of a young woman, one of the *munaqqabas,* performing her ablutions prior to the dawn prayer. At the foot of the wall I saw the aluminium plate, covered by the loaf, and surrounded by scurrying cockroaches and beetles which disappeared into the cracks of the wall the minute they sensed a foot striking adjacent ground. I saw her leaning over the plate, and I heard her chewing on the bread. Swallowing a bit of water, she whispered to herself, 'Hunger leads to disbelief.'

Now, at the base of the wall, in the same spot, I stumbled over a loaf which was old and dry as a disc of cement. I snatched it from the ground and returned at a run to the courtyard. I did not see them – those two coals in a skull. I saw her back, bent, as she half-ran, half-limped, followed by the *shawisha* waving a cane. 'Don't go near the political prisoners' cell, you beggar, you beggar's daughter! God take you and relieve the prison of your presence!'

She flashed the cane, spat on the ground, wiped her mouth with her palm. She entered the enclosure, followed closely by her aide, Dhuba, who carried a tall pile of loaves on her chest, with a large aluminium plate balanced on top.

Her smile revealing two rows of small, very white teeth in a strikingly dark face, Dhuba called out in a merry voice, 'Forty-two loaves, exactly three apiece. The plate is full to the brim with *ful*. This is all for the sake of Mama Nabawiyya and for the good of you all, political women.'

I took a loaf from her chest and scurried towards the door of the enclosure. From afar, I saw those black irises gleaming in the vast space, concealed behind a wall. Her head would poke out and then disappear again, her eyes would shine for a fleeting moment and vanish, like two stars glittering before they are extinguished.

I called out in a loud voice: 'Come over here. Don't hide away.'

Shawisha Nabawiyya heard my voice from inside the cell, where she and Dhuba were distributing the loaves to my cellmates. At a run, she came up to me. 'Please, doctor . . . you're not allowed to speak to the prisoners. The Internal Security police officer will arrive at any time, and if he sees her speaking to you, well, the day won't turn out well for any of us.'

'This woman is practically dying of hunger,' I said. 'Look at her eyes, look at how a hungry fire burns in them.'

'Do you really believe she'll take the loaf in order to eat it?' asked the *shawisha*. 'She'll throw it in the garbage pail, then sit and scratch at the dirt and eat that. She's mad. Look how she's laughing, there in the distance, look, and she only has three teeth in her mouth.'

The *shawisha* spread out a blanket on the floor of the enclosure and sat down. I stood next to her, observing the woman through the bars of the door. I saw her sit down on the ground, scratching at the dust with her long fingernails and singing at the top of her voice,

Ahh, these are the times that torment the one who has gone their way
And have moistened bitter aloe in the cup, giving him to drink as they wish.

The *shawisha* laughed. 'God take you, girl, Sabah. By the Prophet, you belong in the madhouse, not in the prison.'

I squatted beside the *shawisha* and leaned my back against the wall. 'Why is she in prison?' I asked. 'What's her crime?'

'Begging.' Nabawiyya replied. 'She gets out of prison and goes to beg in Cairo, in the neighbourhood of Sayyida Zaynab. Then she comes back into prison, begging and going back and forth in the courtyard all day long, all night too, limping, or she sits there, scratching at the ground and singing. A crazy woman – her mind's flown right off. She was here, in the beggar's cell, before any of you arrived. We emptied this cell for you. Now the beggarwomen have only a tiny hut in the big courtyard, a hut which isn't large enough for all of them. They lie down to sleep in the courtyard. Sometimes, one of them pees all over herself as she's sitting or lying down. Their life would draw sympathy even from an unbeliever. Except for this madwoman. Listen to what she's singing. Her voice sounds as unhappy as the screech of an owl.'

I pricked up my ears so as to catch the lyrics of the song. Her hoarse voice, full of an awesome grief, began loud and grew faint, as if the vocal chords were being worn down or shredded, then it got louder again like the playing of a taut string, only to grow sweeter and softer until breaking off so that I could hear just the harsh sound of fitful, intermittent breathing.

Ahh, these are the times that torment the one who has gone their way
And have moistened bitter aloe in the cup, giving him to drink as they wish
And this is the upright maiden, into prison thrown
And the son of the bitch gives orders and does as he pleases . . .[1]

The *shawisha* let out a loud laugh: 'God's curses upon you, Sabah. *Ibn al-hafiyya* . . . the son of the bitch gives orders and does as he pleases . . . Ahh, if only the Internal Security police officer could hear you!'

One of the young *munaqqabas* had come out of the cell, a copy of the Qur'an in her hands. 'Who's that? *Ibn al-hafiyya*?' she inquired, as she sat down beside the *shawisha*.

'I don't know – ask the doctor.' Her eyes filled with tears, the result of so much laughter, and she wiped them away, saying, 'Let's hope for the best. May God make our words light upon their hearts . . . upon them.'

'Them? Who are they?' asked the girl.

The *shawisha* said, still laughing. 'The souls of jinnis, my girl. This prison is full of the souls of jinnis.'

The girl raised the *niqaab* from over her mouth and spat into the opening of her cloak, saying, 'God spare us their evil.'

The prison chimney began to hurl its thick, black smoke over us. The *shawisha* was still chuckling, her breathing cut short by a suppressed laughter which sounded more like sobbing. She wiped her eyes, grown watery with so much laughter, on a white handkerchief which she drew out of the pocket of her grey overcoat, swiped at her forehead, nose and cheeks, then unrolled the handkerchief. It had gone black.

She stopped laughing and said sorrowfully, 'May your day be black, Sabah, like your face and like this black soot which the chimney heaps on us every day. Oh Lord, when will You show Your mercy to me and get me out of this prison?'

Dhuba had come out of the cell. She stopped next to the *shawisha*, her feet bare, her tall thin figure cased in a white robe which was open at the chest, revealing a deep cleavage between her full breasts. Gesturing towards the sky, she called out, 'O Lord, when will You show Your mercy to us, all of us?'

The veiled girl raised her eyes from the Qur'an. 'God will show

---

[1]These lines follow the form of a folk/traditional poem-song type known as *mawwal*, which is composed in colloquial Arabic and relies heavily on paronomasia and double meanings. Examples in this quatrain: *sabr*, 'aloe' (metaphor for bitterness) is also 'patience'; *balbal*, 'he moistened' also can take the meaning 'to confuse'.

His mercy to you when you begin to wear the *niqaab*.'

Dhuba laughed as she sat down on the ground. 'Lord, if I'm given my release in tomorrow's court session, I'll put on the *niqaab* and repent.'

The *shawisha* clapped her on the shoulder. 'By God, even if all the prostitutes were to repent, Dhuba wouldn't. She's a bastard child, and so was her father.'

'No, Mama Nabawiyya,' remonstrated Dhuba, 'Say whatever you like but leave my father out of it. He was a good man, an honest, upright one. The bastard was my husband, God take him and his likes from us all.'

She drew a cigarette from her *gallabiyya* pocket. Gazing fixedly at the sky, she blew the smoke from her nostrils. Her head was raised, revealing a long brown neck gleaming in the light, like a neck of ebony belonging to a statue in a museum, the head of a black youth from the eras of slavery.

The stretch of sky visible over the walls was covered by a greyish cloud, the colour of smoke. Through it pierced the sun's rays, to pass across the wires and fall on to the wall, scattering over the stone protuberances, twisting with the cracks, coming to rest in the form of a circle of gold beside my feet as I sat on the ground, the loaf of bread still in my lap, while Sabah the beggar scratched at the ground and sang.

I stretched out my feet. The ray hitting my leg burned hotly like a tongue of flame. I drew back my leg, raised my hand and began to move it back and forth like a fan. But the air was still; none was entering my nostrils. Instead, small black specks scorched the upper part of my nose and flew scattered through the air like bits of sand in a black desert or watery drizzle in a sea of tar.

I wiped my face with my white handkerchief, and it went black. The hoarse voice was still ringing in my ears, and the words were borne over the hot air in the tones of a braying, slaughtered animal, moving with the motes of black smoke and invading my ears like a flow of poison gas under pressure.

Patience is all wisdom, what was unclear now is clear
On the outside well-adorned, and inside full of smoke
Be patient, my love, to everything there is a time.

I heard a strange sound next to me, like the sucking of hundreds of lips at an immense funeral. I observed my veiled cellmates sitting on the ground, their backs to the wall and their heads bowed over their chests, lips moving in that bizarre sucking movement.

One girl raised her black-veiled head toward the sky and spoke. 'To everything there is a time, and we will not leave here until the proper time comes, through the permission of God.' The others called out in unison, 'Everything is by God's permission.'

The voice of Fathiyya-the-Murderess rang out from behind the bars of the door: 'Open up, Nabawiyya.' A tall woman, dressed in the white regulation *gallabiyya* of the prisoners, entered the enclosure and the *shawisha* locked the door behind her. She lifted a tray from her head and placed it on the ground in front of the *shawisha*. Her movements resembled those of my cousin Nafisa raising the water jug off her head and placing it on the ground without spilling even a single drop of water. Strong bones and strong muscles, a proudly-raised head. She drew the cover from the tray to reveal a large shallow bowl brimming with *mulukhiyya* – a soup of greens – not a single drop of which had been spilled. Another plate held a grilled chicken, boiled potatoes, pickled aubergine, peppered rice and two loaves of bread. There was also a cup of tea full to the top from which not a single drop had fallen, a pitcher of water, soap, and a hand towel.

The *shawisha* rolled up the sleeves of her coat and washed her hands. She grasped the chicken, murmuring, 'In the name of God the merciful and compassionate. Help yourselves, my ladies.'

The cell inhabitants replied in unison, 'Eat in good health and satisfaction.'

The *shawisha* became engrossed in eating. On her right squatted Fathiyya-the-Murderess, waving flies away with the towel. Dhuba arose to sweep the cell and toilets. My veiled cellmates remained sitting in their usual places on the ground, backs supported against the wall, eyes on the Qur'an, and lips moving quickly and noiselessly.

No one paid attention to her as she approached the bars of the door. I noticed two coals aflame like stars glittering, and I extended my arm to push the loaf through the bars. She snatched it with her long fingers, the tips ending in nails pointed like the claws of a kite.

She opened her mouth, revealing three small front teeth, the mouth of a child whose teeth have not yet completely grown. Her eyes shone with a childlike sparkle. She broke out with a moaning laugh and turned to run, limping and singing.

The voice of Sabah the beggar, as she sings, reminds my of my aunt Zaynab's voice.

I was a student in secondary school in 1948 when Aunt Zaynab died of cholera. I remember hearing her sing as she sat on the earthen floor of the courtyard in the family home, her back supported against the wall, nursing the child in her lap. After Zaynab died, my grandmother took her place, holding the child in her lap, singing to him, and offering him a skinny breast which held not one drop of milk.

The dirt enclosure here reminds me of the courtyard of my grandmother's house. The rural dialect of the prisoners is like that spoken in my native village, Kafr Tahla, and so are the bare cracked feet and emaciated brown hands. The memories of my childhood form one long extended image, past to present, unbound by time, unbroken by dividing intervals. The picture ends suddenly, as if severed at the face of my daughter, or son, or husband: three faces which no longer take shape in my mind, even as I sleep.

It is just like a screen image, closing in on my home, almost revealing one of those faces, or even one of their backs, just before the picture is cut off suddenly, as if the hand of the censor has extended with scissors open. A hand of iron, like my will. . . and my decision is as sharply defined as the edge of a knife, a conscious decision which my mind – both accessible and subconscious – brings forth: to live in prison as if this has been my life since birth and will be so until I die. I'll hold no hopes for tomorrow other than the expectation that I will open my eyes upon these same four walls and find them slightly less black, their cracks and holes grown narrower and closing up to swallow the jagged-legged creatures. The stopped-up toilet openings will no longer be blocked, and the shower holes will open, allowing water to fall in thick streams, while the hole in the chimney will grow narrower until it is fully closed and blocked.

During the first few days in prison, my anticipation of the future did not extend beyond the walls of the cell – and the toilet. Going out into the small dirt enclosure broadened my hopes to include the surrounding walls. I would gaze from between the steel bars on the door to the large prison courtyard and I'd sense my hopes creeping out into that wide space, all the way over to that large tree with its spreading branches and soft green leaves. Maybe tomorrow my fingers would touch them.

When I thought of the future, my mind did not extend beyond the walls of the enclosure or those of the courtyard. Every time I opened my eyes to a new day and saw some part of our hopes for the future come to fruition, in the toilet or cell, a sense of optimism and happiness would come over me. When the shower was put in and the abundant drizzles of water fell on my body for the first time since I'd entered prison, I began to sing an old tune which I'd loved since I was a child. As I washed my hair, the scent of the soap and the taste of the water had a sweetness of which I had not been conscious since my childhood, and the feel of the water on my body was as strongly pleasurable as if I had not had a bath since I was a child. My voice, too, took on a sweetness of tone which resounded in my ears as if I had not sung since I was little.

I heard the voice from outside the toilet's half-open broken door, and I saw the two small openings in the black *niqaab*. One hand inside a black glove went up rapidly to cover the two eyeholes while the other plugged an ear, and I heard her say, 'May God Almighty forgive our sins. Singing is taboo.'

My eyes widened in astonishment. Even my maternal grandmother used to sing, although she was born to a Turkish mother and lived in my grandfather's house in the epoch when harems still existed. I never saw her hair uncovered, nor did I see her leave the house until she was borne away inside a coffin. Yet, I used to listen to her singing as she sat in her spacious sitting room on soft cushions, her wool-stockinged feet stretched out on the intricately woven Persian carpet and her head wrapped in a white veil which quivered as she sang. My grandfather – stern military man, zealous son of a religious shaykh – would pass by as she sat and listen to her sing without ever once saying to her that singing was taboo.

Through the drizzle of water, the shape standing behind the shutter of the broken door, her head and body wrapped in black, one black hand on her ear and the other over her eyes, appeared to me like a stone statue from earlier times, those of feudalism and slavery.

A dream would tease me as I stood behind the steel door peering between the bars at the prisoners walking in the vast courtyard. I dreamed that I would open my eyes and find that I was one of them, that I too was strolling through that extended courtyard as far as the huge, thickly-branched tree with its green leaves flashing and trembling, perceivable even from a distance.

Hearing my wish, the *shawisha* rapped her chest with a cracked brown hand. 'May evil remain far from you, doctor. Those women out there are all from the cells of the prostitutes, drug traffickers, pickpockets and beggars, and they're all bitches.'

Laughing, I replied, 'But they are free to walk as they wish in the courtyard while we are caged in here.'

'The longest day has an end. Just two or three weeks and the difficult period will be over. And then, what's in the courtyard after all? Nothing more than there is in this enclosure. Dirt and more dirt.'

'There's a tree.'

Fathiyya-the-Murderess, waving flies away from the plates in front of the *shawisha*, sighed. 'You've got a point, doctor. I go over to that tree every day and sit beneath it as if I'm sitting in the field in front of our house in the village.'

The *shawisha* struck her on the shoulder, laughing as she did so. 'That's because you're a peasant and daughter of a peasant, but she's a doctor – she's not familiar with the field or the house in your poor country town.'

Her laugh resembled that of my peasant grandmother, the mother of my father.

Fathiyya's small eyes gazed at the *shawisha*. Only now did I see those eyes fully; a glittering brightness to dazzle one's eyes and a strong, steady gaze. Only now did I comprehend that she might be capable of murder: previously, I had thought that she had been unable even to kill a gnat.

'Our poor country town, Nabawiyya?' she said. 'Poor *shawisha*!'

The *shawisha* went on as if uninterrupted. 'We're all poor, all the peasants are poor, and poverty is nothing to be ashamed of. Nothing's a shame except shame itself.'

Fathiyya laughed. 'No shame but the Law of Shame. Isn't that so, doctor?'

'By God, Fathiyya, I believe you're right,' I said.

They call her Fathiyya-the-Murderess. Since women in the prison often have similar or identical names, the prisoners distinguish between one individual and another according to her crime or the charge against her, which is then added to her name like a family identity. They say Fathiyya-the-Murderess, or Fathiyya-the-Prostitute, or Fathiyya-the-Drugpusher, or Fathiyya-the-Thief, or Fathiyya-the-Political Activist.

Fathiyya-the-Murderess would astonish me sometimes with her strong, svelte movements, her confident voice, and her caustic talk – or with that gleam which would clothe her eyes and remind me of Zaynab, my peasant cousin.

'I have a cousin who looks just like you, Fathiyya.'

She laughed. 'A doctor like you, or a peasant like me?'

'She's a peasant, but she has a doctor's brain. She was with me in elementary school. She was top of the class but her father married her off to her peasant cousin. My father's mother, a peasant, wanted to marry me to my cousin, also a peasant. If I'd married him I would have been a peasant too, exactly like her, working the fields with a hoe.'

'It's wonderful to work with a hoe in the fields,' Fathiyya breathed. 'I can't live without a hoe. It's my life and has been since I came out of my mother's belly.'

'But after all,' commented the *shawisha* with a laugh, 'you're a murderess and the daughter of one. Doctor, this Fathiyya who sits in front of you, wearing a smile like that of the angels, gave her husband a blow on the head with her hoe then cut up his body into little pieces which she gathered in a sack and threw into the river so the fishes would eat him.'

Fathiyya laughed. 'Why shouldn't the fish eat him? At least that way he has a last use in the world – he can wipe out his sins before he meets his maker face to face.'

She sprang up from where she sat on the ground, raising the bottom of her *gallabiyya* to reveal strong leg muscles. She walked towards the door, striking the ground audibly with her bare feet and rolling up the sleeves of her *gallabiyya* to bare her strong arms: 'Open the door for me, Nabawiyya. Nothing worse in the world than sitting around like this uselessly.' Her small eyes swept across the *munaqqabas*, sitting fast against the wall, concealed under veils and black cloaks, their gloved hands firmly placed on the Qur'ans in their laps.

She tossed her arm in their direction. 'What's wrong with you, my girls? Wrapped up in black shrouds before the time has come.'

Gazing at Fathiyya's bare arms and legs, one of them replied, 'It's a sin to show your arms and legs like that.' Fathiyya bent over and touched her legs. 'My arms and legs. . . are pretty. Why should I cover them? Open the door, Nabawiyya, I want to get out of here. I have a lot of work to do.'

Dhuba, too, uncovered her arms and legs and said, 'Mama Fathiyya, I have pretty arms and legs too.'

Slapping Dhuba across the shoulders, the *shawisha* handed her the two large keys: 'Get up now, open the door for your Mama Fathiyya. You're black as slave girls ever were, and I don't know how you can work your trade when you're just skin and bones, no flesh at all on that body of yours.'

Dhuba rose, stretching her neck in pride and blowing the smoke from her nostrils. 'I don't work the trade, Mama Nabawiyya. I have my own flat and three girls. I'm a proper madam, and you know it.'

She opened the door and Fathiyya-the-Murderess went out. Locking the door behind Fathiyya, Dhuba came back to sit beside the *shawisha*.

Nabawiyya slapped her again. 'I don't know anything about you or about anyone with you over there in the prostitute's cell. God keep us separate. I know only the respectable women in the political cell.'

The *shawisha* looked at us, one after the other, as if counting. Suddenly she let out a yell. 'Calamity! I've had it now! There are only 13 of you! Where's number 14?'

The voice of the young girl came from inside the cell: 'I'm in here, *shawisha*, sweeping out the cell.'

The *shawisha* struck Dhuba on the shoulder again and said, 'Get up, Dhuba, now dust the cell and the toilet and do the laundry.'

Dhuba withdrew the cigarette butt from her mouth and extinguished it with a bare foot. She glanced across at us. 'Who has
clothes she wants washed?'

I'd not given her any clothes at all to launder. After my morning
exercises I would wash out my clothes and spread them on the line
in the enclosure before the sun could flee, disappearing over the
wall. I was accustomed to washing my clothes by hand: I'd only had
an automatic washer for two years. In prison, I discovered a bizarre
enjoyment in washing my clothes and spreading them out on the
rope, piece by piece, under the sun.

I didn't have any clothes pegs, and a single gust of wind would
send the clothes flying to land on the dirty floor. I would pick them
up and re-wash them. Whenever the chimney began to belch,
specks of soot would fly over the line, falling like scattered black
stains on the clothes. I would take them back to the basin for
re-washing.

All my life, I'd loathed repetition and been bored by it. But in
prison I did not tire of washing my clothes time after time, my arms
plunged in the water and foam up to the elbow, rubbing the clothes
vigorously, squeezing them strongly, then spreading them out on
the line, piece by piece, stretched out to the utmost so they would
dry quickly. I would sit nearby with my gaze upon them. If
something were to slip off the line, I'd run to grab it before it could
touch the ground. If it hit before I could reach it I would roll it into a
ball in my hands and run inside the cell to wash it again in the
bucket. Then I'd come back, spread it out on the line and sit down
once again, my arms alert and moving constantly from one end of
the clothes line to the other, picking out the black soot flying in the
air before it could land on the piece of clothing. Seeing the tiny
motes of soot moving in front of my eye, I would brace my neck
muscles to fix my head in place as if I were looking through a
microscope, and trying to steady my gaze over the black circles
which swam in the light like the round shapes of cells under my eyes
in the laboratory of the College of Medicine. But only moments
would pass before my eyes would move far from the clothes drying
on the line to pierce the bars of the door, traversing it to reach the
vast courtyard.

A short, thin woman, her hair short and frizzy, her face showing the traces of old wounds, was beckoning to me. But the sharp voice of the *shawisha* rang out loudly: 'Go away, you thief, daughter of a thief, talking to the political prisoners is prohibited.'

Not a single thing escaped the eyes of the *shawisha*, who spent most of her time sitting in the enclosure, her cracked and skinny legs extended for Dhuba to massage with her small, soft, brown hands. The *shawisha* would close her eyes: seeing her, one would think that she was asleep but she would in fact be seeing everything from beneath those half-shut lids.

'What do you have to say in the novel, doctor?' I heard her say abruptly.

'What novel?!!'

She winked at me. 'The novel you're writing here in prison.'

I laughed. 'I write in my memory, since I have no paper and pen.'

'Doctor' – this from Dhuba – 'Are you a doctor of medicine or writing?'

The *shawisha* replied. 'She's a doctor of medicine and writing both, but she's only accused of writing. She's got nothing to do with the religious groups, or the communist parties either. They say you've written things against Sadat. Is that true, doctor?'

'Against Sadat personally?' Dhuba's black eyes gleamed.

'Not against him personally,' I said. 'I don't write against anyone personally. I have my own views and ideas. There is meant to be democracy in the country and it's the right of every individual to write his or her opinion freely.'

'Naturally,' commented the *shawisha*, 'people must write their own opinions and speak the truth. But everyone gets afraid and keeps quiet. And anyway – what's the point of writing? Doctor, is writing of any use? What's writing? Just words on paper, and that's it, and all you get for it is an entrance to prison. Anyway, generally speaking, it's all a matter of our assigned lot in life, and ours is to oversee you and your cellmates. You're all respectable people. Only respectable people get into political cells, whether in the women's prison or the men's. In the men's cell I've seen Ministers – and more than Ministers – and among political women I've seen respectable ladies. One of them still visits me every year at the festival time and brings me and my ten kids presents. A decent person can't possibly forget the companionship of prison. The political cells are all good, solid folk, but as for the other cells . . . thieves, beggars, prostitutes, drugpushers – all of them have bastard backgrounds. Except the murderesses. They're the best ones. A murderess comes straight from her home to prison, doesn't even know the meaning of dodging or evading. Murder is unlike all other crimes – in fact, it isn't a crime, but a moment of anger which passes. The murderess kills for the sake of her children and her honour. But the thieves, prostitutes and drugpushers, well, they walk the streets, here and there, come into prison and leave prison 20 times, and not one of them is capable in the least of repenting or finding God. Not a chance she'll admit that's she's done something wrong. Everyone who enters this prison says, "I haven't done anything wrong".'

Sitting close by, on the lead-coloured blanket, I followed her words. Between my fingers was a sharp bit of rock with which I was drawing in the dirt, sketching the *shawisha*'s head in profile.

She took a square white bone comb out of her pocket and handed it to Dhuba. She untied the white kerchief round her head and Dhuba began combing her short frizzy hair as she went on speaking.

'If she hasn't done anything wrong, then why have the police grabbed her, specifically, out of all God's creatures on earth? She must have done something. But there are people who come into prison who've been wronged themselves. Ahh, how many wrongs are done in prison! The down-and-out folk come into prison because they're in a miserable state of poverty. An innocent and uneducated woman, for instance, who knows nothing at all – but it's the innocent and ignorant one who gets put into prison. They pass sentences on the innocent, naïve woman, while the one who knows how things work can't possibly fall into this situation, even if it's a question of political action. Three years ago, a woman came here, into the political cell, who was a real innocent, knew nothing at all about politics. It was just a case of mistaken identity, and they locked up the innocent woman. The other one, who took care, escaped. Do you know how many months it took to correct that mistake and get the first one released? Three months, by God. And then there was another one, who had nothing to do with political work at all. Her husband is a political activist – they arrested him and put him in prison. On him they found a letter from his wife in which she'd written, "I'm with you, darling, as long as I live." Well, they arrested her and put her in gaol. Lots of them over in the murderesses' cell are wronged, too. A man kills someone and escapes, so his mother or his wife or sister enters prison. A mother tries to save her son, by claiming that she was the murderess. The wife, too, gives herself in sacrifice for her husband. A man escapes from the army, so they grab his mother and wife. A man pushes his wife into working as a prostitute or into pushing drugs, and it's she who gets put into prison. Women have it rotten, doctor. They go to prison for the sake of others. Even Sabah the beggar – when she comes to prison, it's because one of Sadat's important guests is on his way to Egypt. The police scurry around collecting her and her likes from the streets. They sweep the streets clean of garbage and beggars so that the important guest will say that our country is clean. Sabah comes to prison for a fortnight and gets out . . . comes in again, and leaves again. Her situation would make even a disbeliever feel sorry for her. There are lots of other examples, too; even here in the political cell, where a woman may come in and then get out soon after, but they'll grab her again whenever anything happens in the country. Even that innocent girl who came in because of a mistake over names: from the day she came in they wrote her name wrong in the lists here. Every time there is a strike or a demonstration they arrest her. They grab her with the communists, and with the Islamic groups, when she's neither a communist nor a Muslim. Her father is a Christian and her mother is Muslim but her luck is bad and the only refuge is God. I mean, did her name really have to be Widad Ibrahim Fawzi? Could be the name of a Christian woman, or a Muslim, or a communist or even a Jew. But her luck is rotten. It's all a question of luck. No woman who has good luck can enter prison, just like you'll never see a woman go to prison who has backing somewhere, or a man who can protect her, or land or money. It's not a question of rights or justice or courts or a judge. Money is everything. Someone who's further up on the ladder than she is in the drug business, or in prostitution, or whatever, comes out innocent right away. Or even if she does go to prison, she'll just spend a short bit of time there, and she'll live like a queen while she's inside.'

Dhuba was moving the bone comb through the *shawisha*'s coarse hair, scraping the skin of her skull and then drawing the comb out to pick a black louse from between its fine teeth. She'd put the louse on the surface of the white comb and press it with the nail of her big toe: a light crunch, a bit of red blood showing against the white.

Still holding the sharp bit of rock between my fingers, I was inscribing letters and meaningless words in the dirt, my handwriting awkwardly crooked as it was when I was a child.

The *shawisha* lay on her side, Dhuba beside her head combing her hair, picking out the lice, and smiling in pleasure every time she found a new louse among the teeth. The *shawisha* scratched her head and went on. 'Ah, doctor, if only you'd seen Hagga Badia in the drugpushers' cell![1] Goes right to one's heart, she does. And living like a queen, has everything with her right in prison, even a colour TV. Here in the gaol she makes several times the profit she can make outside, but it's all due to God's providence. Profit comes from God, loss comes from God. If Our Lord wants to make someone happy He gives him the wealth of Midas. It's all the Lord's judgement and wisdom – only gives to those who deserve it. And Hagga Badia deserves every blessing that comes to her. She has a good heart, she's generous. She gives alms to the poor and prays and fasts and keeps her heart close to our Lord. At festival time she has animals slaughtered in the proper religious way and distributes them among the cells, and the whole prison eats well. I was with her in the drugs cell last year, and from that day she's always sent me a tray of food. But it is all from God, and it's all a question of our lot.'

I found myself writing on the ground with the tip of the little rock: mistake in a name, three months. The *shawisha*'s eyes, as she reclined there, followed the movement of my hand over the dirt. She shook her head. 'If the Internal Security police officer were to show up right now in the courtyard and see from a distance that you are writing, he'd think you have some paper and a pen. Nothing on his mind but pens and paper. He calls me into his office just to ask me about that, and I swear to him by the greatness of God that in the entire political cell there is not a single scrap of paper or a pen.

[1] *Hagg/Hagga*: term of respect for an elderly man/woman. Originally (and still) the title given to those who have made the pilgrimage to Mecca, which is the duty of every Muslim – who is able to do so – once in his or her life.

But he won't believe me. He is always suspicious, and he begins from early morning prowling around the prison. He has no work, nothing else to keep him busy. If he sees a lame woman or even a blind one looking towards the political cell he'll grab her and search her, or he'll call in the female warder or *shawisha* to strip off all her clothes and give her a body search. And woe to her if they find a cigarette paper on which something is written with a normal pencil or with an eyebrow pencil. Any sort of writing implement, and that's that. Or any written words. A couple of words like 'How are things?' That is, any old meaningless phrase and they raise hell. She'd go to hell and so would the *shawisha*, because the *shawisha* is responsible. The *shawisha* is even worse off than the prisoner. But the important thing is that not even one piece of paper should be around, since not one written word can possibly leave or enter the political cell. In the other cells, it's possible – any cell but this one. One written word in the political cell is a more serious matter than having a pistol. Writing is more dangerous than killing, doctor. Killing, according to the way we see things here, is the simplest matter of all, and the murderers are the best people. They've all had miserable lives. Fathiyya-the-Murderess was a poor miserable woman, planting and harvesting with her own hands, while her husband lounged around the house, a lazy bum. Eating, burping, smoking his waterpipe. One day, she came back from the field and found him on top of her daughter, her nine-year-old daughter. She struck him on the head with her hoe and got a life sentence. She's been with us here for ten years now. Her heart is as sweet and gentle as the spring breeze, and it's impossible to believe that she would kill a mosquito. But her luck is bad. Our Lord gave her a man who was a bastard. If Our Lord had given her a good man, she'd be at home, on her own land, her daughter in her arms. It's all according to the lot we get in life.'

At that moment, Dhuba's fingers were going after a louse hidden between the teeth of the comb. She raised her black eyes towards the sky and said, 'If Our Lord had given me a respectable man who hadn't made me work as a prostitute I'd be home in my own flat now, holding my little girl. And if Our Lord had given Sabah-the-Beggar a respectable man she'd be at home hugging her children. If Our Lord had given Souad-the-Thief an upstanding father who hadn't forced her into stealing she'd be a respectable matron in her own home by now. Behind every woman who's entered prison there's a real son of a bitch. Father, husband, brother, uncle, cousin. Any man. But its Our Lord who gives, and everything is according to lot.'

The *shawisha* gave her a slap across the shoulders. 'Our Lord never told any woman to steal or work as a prostitute or sell drugs. Our Lord provides according to what is right, but he gave minds to human beings so they could know right from wrong. Take my situation. Our Lord gave me a poor father who'd never been to school or learnt to read and write but I have a brain which tells me such-and-such is right, and such-and-such is wrong, and because of that I turned out as a *shawisha*. Why didn't I turn out to be a thief or a prostitute like you, Dhuba, hmm? You types do all sorts of damage and then you say "It's all from Our Lord." Well, its not Our Lord's fault.'

Dhuba tossed the comb to the ground, a louse still between its teeth, and flung her head in the air.

'Yes, from Our Lord. Everything is by the will of Our Lord. It was His will that I became a prostitute, so I did. If He'd wanted me to be a doctor I'd have been a doctor.' Dhuba looked at me. 'What d'you think, doctor?'

I was still moving my fingers, the pointed bit of rock between them, over the ground. I found myself drawing two squares. Inside the first one I wrote 'Our Lord is not at fault' and inside the second, 'Our Lord is at fault.'

The *shawisha's* small eyes contemplated the letters on the ground. 'What did you write?'

I laughed. 'I wrote that it's Sadat, first and foremost, who is responsible.'

The *shawisha* struck herself on the chest. 'Catastrophe! If the Internal Security policeman shows up right now and reads what you've written, why, I'll have hell to pay.' She extended her gaunt brown hand and wiped out the letters in the dirt, saying, 'What's the use of writing, doctor? Words and more words, and all you get for it is prison, while Sadat perches up there in the sky, more like a king than Farouq was in his own time. Even if he asks the impossible . . .'

74

She raised her half-closed eyes towards the sky, and in the same instant the birds perched on the barbed wire lit out into the sky in an agitated flurry which suggested fright. The walls trembled with a thunderlike sound, as if an earthquake had just taken place. The sky was eclipsed by a helicopter which circled above our heads for a fleeting moment before it disappeared. I saw only its greyish belly, glistening in the sun like the pregnant stomach of a huge water beast or a crazed mythical insect with wings turning in its head.

The *shawisha* jumped up, pounded on the ground with a bare foot which she jammed quickly into a slipper, then knocked one cracked heel against the other and raised her hand, fingers rigid against her forehead in the military or police salute familiar since the era of the Turkish sultans and Mamluks.

'Sadat,' she breathed.

The sky became peaceful once again, and the birds came back to alight on the barbed wires. The *shawisha* returned to her place and sat tying up her hair in the kerchief, still speaking in a hushed voice: 'Sadat has just left his rest home in the Barrages. What a mess I'd be in if he'd heard me! I'd be in hell already, ahh, Nabawiyya, you clever girl.'

Dhuba motioned upward. 'How could Sadat hear you when he's up in the sky?' She, too, had jumped to her feet when she heard the helicopter's motor. My cellmates had rushed out into the enclosure, raising their eyes skywards.

The *shawisha* tossed a small clod of hard earth at Dhuba and said, 'Shut up, girl, shut up, Dhuba. You don't know anything. I'm a *shawisha* and I know more than you do . . . the ants crawling over the ground here' – the *shawisha* struck the ground with her palm – 'the ants crawling over this spot can be heard anywhere in the sky or the earth. The world has progressed, and everything is possible. A respected doctor – like you, doctor – said one word to her husband while lying in bed, in her own home. Next day, she was here in prison with me. Long ago, when we were children, we used to laugh at my mother if she said "The walls have ears" but Nabawiyya, you've lived, you've seen with your own eyes that walls do have ears, indeed they do.'

She moved her small unlashed eyes over the walls, searching and examining them, squinting with one eye. My *munaqqaba* cellmates had come to sit in their usual places in the enclosure, leaning their backs against the wall. Through the narrow slits in the large expanses of blackness, small eyes roved the walls and they called out in unison, 'God is over all.'

Reclining once again on her side, the *shawisha* asked me, 'Have you seen Sadat in person?'

'Yes.'

'How many times?'

'Two or three, I don't remember exactly.'

'Did you talk to him?'

'They were large gatherings, and I didn't speak with him, but I spoke in the meeting.'

Her eyes were closed, as if dozing, but she asked 'What meeting?' Her eyes remained shut. She must have drifted off to sleep. I studied her long dark face.

Suddenly, she opened her eyes wide and she said in a voice of wonder, 'What did you say to Sadat?'

I laughed. 'Nothing. Go to sleep, *shawisha*, and I'll watch the door for you.' She smiled and closed her eyes once again.

I remembered that day, years ago . . . it must have been earlier than 1970 because Gamal Abdel Nasser was still alive. I was invited to attend one of the large group meetings of the Socialist Union; this particular one was held for hundreds of members of the various professional bodies. I was a member of the Council of the Physicians' Syndicate, and I took my seat like the others, waiting for the arrival of the senior Socialist Union officials.

We numbered roughly three hundred or more doctors, lawyers, engineers and others from various professions in Egypt. We sat for over two hours, waiting for someone to appear on the large platform in the main hall of the Socialist Union.

This was my first meeting with these top aides of Nasser's. I said to the colleague sitting next to me, 'The meeting was scheduled for 11 a.m., and it's now after one. Something serious must have happened to prevent them from attending.' I got the strangest response I could possibly have heard. In a calm voice which suggested that he was accustomed to this situation he replied: 'They're always late like this.'

'Incredible!! Why are all these people waiting then?'

The same calm voice: 'They're afraid to leave.'

'I can't believe it!'

Our conversation was cut off by a general stir of people rising to their feet, and applause, and I saw Anwar Sadat – then Deputy to the President of the Republic – come in, followed by the senior government and Socialist Union men. They sat down on the platform. Sadat opened the meeting without offering one word of justification or explanation for the delay. I understood that my colleague had been right when he had told me that they were always late like this.

Sadat finished what he had to say, and the dialogue commenced between him and those present. Some of the syndicate presidents spoke out but no one brought up the subject of the delay. Others spoke, but said nothing about the delay either. I understood the soundness of my colleague's words when he'd said they were afraid to leave. So why speak at all then?

I raised my hand and requested the floor. I began my comments thus: 'Mr Anwar Sadat has spoken of the struggle. He said that economies of war call for saving in every sphere, hard work everywhere, and increased production in all sectors, but I noticed today that more than three hundred individuals were prevented from working for over two hours as they were waiting for your entrance to this hall. It appears that this is the usual procedure in these meetings, since you mentioned nothing about the reasons for this delay. I request that we calculate, in the language of economics and mathematical figures, the amount lost to the state and to the national income from this sort of delay.'

Then I spoke on other points having to do with spurious slogans and the absence of democracy. I was speaking calmly, and supporting my observations with real examples through which we've lived. I don't have any recollection of what Sadat said in reply. But he did not address the points to which I had spoken. He also ignored the subject of the delay. He made some general comments to the effect that I was demanding perfection or fulfilment of an ideal, but that an ideal – or the attainment of perfection – are attributes of God alone, His praises be sung.

I was astonished at this response, and so were all of those present, I believe, since I had not been demanding perfection but rather a minimum level of respect for the individual Egyptian – not to mention large groups of people who are wronged by waiting in meeting halls and prevented from carrying on production.

Before the meeting was over, I felt a hand on my sleeve, and a high-ranking official from the Ministry of the Interior called me over to meet a more senior official from the same Ministry. That official said to me: 'We are in the middle of a struggle and we do not want any criticism at the moment.'

'But the struggle demands objective criticism so that the defeat will not be repeated.' My name was inscribed in the list of those who had drawn the ire of the authorities.

The *shawisha* opened her eyes. 'And Sadat's wife?' she asked abruptly. 'Here in prison, they say it was she who goaded her husband into taking a stand against you.'

'Why would she do that, *shawisha*?'

'Don't you know why?' Said with a sly smile.

'I know nothing about it,' I replied. 'How could I, when I'm in prison?'

The *shawisha* rubbed her eyes with a gaunt brown palm. 'They say she gets jealous of any woman who's more beautiful or intelligent than she is. She's Egypt's First Lady, and she doesn't want any woman to surpass her.'

'Who told you this?' I asked.

She stared at me with those small eyes and gave what seemed to me a smile of cunning. 'Doctor, don't you know all of this already?'

'No, I don't.'

'They also say you've written things against her.'

'I don't recall writing anything against her personally. But I'm opposed to having the ruler's wife considered as Egypt's First Lady. This is an imitation of American ways, and I'm against imitation. It's as if the function of the wife – or the ruler's wife – is placed above all other functions or positions. There are Egyptian women who've put in a lot more effort than the wife of the ruler has, and they've got much more of a hold on the hearts and minds of the Egyptian people than she has. A woman should be honoured for her own efforts, not because she is the wife of a man who has influence and power.'

'Every day,' commented the *shawisha*, 'we read in the newspapers about how active she is, and about the great efforts she makes.'

'We didn't hear anything about her activeness until after her husband came to power,' I said. 'And who knows whether she'll be as active after her husband leaves power? What sort of things does she do, anyway? Have her activities really made any difference to the position and circumstances of women? In particular, has this had any effect at all on the problems faced by poor women who work, both at home and outside the home?'

With a dimissive wave of her dark hands, the *shawisha* said, 'Poor people like us are ground down – we have no refuge but God. They say she wears jewels worth thousands of pounds to parties. More jewels than Queen Farida[1] used to wear. By God, doctor, we're a poor, miserable lot, that's got used to humiliation and whippings.'

She glanced around, lips shut tightly. When she next spoke, it was in a suppressed undertone. 'If the walls really do have ears, I'll be sorry.'

Then, laughing, she re-wrapped the kerchief round her head. 'Anyway, even if they hear me, what will they do to me?' She sucked in her lips. 'Can't make things worse for me than they already are in here.' She stared at me with those pale eyes. 'But I'm afraid for you.'

'Don't be, *shawisha*.'

'How can I not be afraid for you? They caused you a lot of harm. I learned that from my niece, who's a student at the College of Medicine. She's read all your books. She found out that they'd fired you from your job, and kept you from being published. They even closed down *Health* Magazine, which she used to read regularly, as well as reading every word you write in the journal of the doctor's syndicate, and in any other newspaper. She followed you when you volunteered to enlist with the Palestinian freedom fighters in Jordan after the 1967 defeat, and in the Canal, and in Ismailia. Not a single thing you write can possibly escape her. When she found out that you were in prison with me here, she wanted to come with me to see you. Her life's wish is to see you. I promised her that as soon as you

---

[1]Queen Farida was the consort of King Farouq, who was deposed following the 1952 Revolution by members of the Egyptian army officer corps.

get out, God willing, the two of us will visit you at home, if God Almighty permits. Lord release you from all this misery, you and all of your cellmates, doctor.'

She raised her hands in supplication, then clutched her head and went on staring into space for a long time as if in silent prayer. Then, with a look in my direction, she broke the silence. 'My niece is always telling me that she'll be a doctor just like you. She wants to be like you in every way.'

I laughed. 'Except in coming to prison.' The *shawisha's* dry lips parted in a smile. 'What's wrong with prison, doctor? In this day and age, by God, prison is an honour! An honour! A blessing and a bountiful grace from our Lord! And what a blessing – thanks O Lord be to Thee.'

She kissed her palm, then the back of her hand – the familiar gesture of humble submission to what has been divinely appointed – before calling out, her voice raised, 'Girl, Dhuba! Where are you?'

Dhuba brought over a bucket of water, a bar of soap and a small stone. The *shawisha* extended her legs and stuck her feet into the bucket. Dhuba began rubbing her cracked feet, which had become black with dust and mud, massaging so vigorously that her small head in its frame of long black hair shook. Between Dhuba's lips was a cigarette, while in profile her raised nose gave her a proud bearing. The smoke emerged from her small nostrils as a tiny black fly landed on the tip of her nose. No – it wasn't a fly, but rather a black speck the size of a lentil, protruding over the skin's surface and growing, unrolling over her prominent cheeks like a black skin rash. She wiped her face on the sleeve of her *gallabiyya*, which turned from white to black. Spitting out her cigarette, she stomped on it with her heel. 'God's curses on the prison and its chimney which pours out tar and crap all over us every morning!'

The *shawisha* filled her cupped palm with water and splattered it across her face. 'Don't say tar and crap. We don't have any tar and crap here. The Barrages Prison is a paradise. If you were to see the other prisons, you'd sing God's praises, thanks be to God, and thank your lucky stars too. Dhuba, girl, you never praise God. When you see the misfortunes of others, your own look small. Ask me. I've seen things that would turn your hair grey. Don't say tar and crap. The chimney works only half the day, and the smoke flies up into the sky. It doesn't corrode or bite or burn the skin or pain the heart. I've seen things that would wring your heart and burn your skin – eyes that cigarettes are put out in, stomachs inflated with air pumps. . . don't say tar and crap. This is luxury here, this is the good life. By God Almighty, it's the good life. But what can we do with human beings: nothing pleases them!'

It's after midnight, now, and I'm seated on top of the overturned bottom of the jerry can, ready to write. Since entering prison I've done my writing on toilet rolls and cigarette papers. Toilet paper isn't against the rules: we buy it from the canteen with our identity cards, like we do cigarettes.

I have not smoked at all since I have been in prison. Outside, I've smoked from time to time, but in here I've decided not to. I've heard of prisoners who've been weakened by a single cigarette, or by one puff of a cigarette. Also, the smoke cuts one's breathing short, and I need deep, long breaths, and all the patience I can muster here, for the struggle ahead of me is still a long one.

In prison, cigarettes become a currency of exchange, a replacement for money. Every service is compensated with a certain number of cigarettes. We gave these to the *shawisha*, and to Dhuba, or to anyone else from the prostitutes' cell who'd been examined by the prison physician and – if cleared of all venereal diseases – was sent to us for a few days and then replaced by someone else. No one stayed with us long: the authorities were afraid of exposing her to our ideas, or to our humanitarian treatment. They were afraid that her loyalty to us would exceed her loyalty to them.

One day, I saw Dhuba heading off with tears in her eyes. 'I won't be coming tomorrow. They want me to spy on all of you, and I refused. I can't turn on you, not after we've had meals together.'[1] I could perceive intelligence, frankness, integrity and honour in the shine of her dark eyes.

'But I can't live without cigarettes,' she added. 'Or pills. What should I do, doctor? If I don't take these drugs, I can't get to sleep

---

[1] This phrase refers to a norm linked to notions of hospitality and trust in Egyptian society: once you have partaken in a meal with someone, a mutual trust is established which cannot be broken.

at all, I'm awake all night. I have to drug myself in order to forget enough to sleep.'

Her tear-filled eyes are still before me. A sharp pain is stabbing at the back of my head like a nail. Pains in my back, as I crouch over the jerry can. My fingers hurt. The pen is an uncomfortable, tiring one – it's so short, shorter than my fingers. The paper is lightweight, and almost transparent. If I press the pen down on it, it rips, and if I don't press down, no letters appear.

The light was dim, and I could barely see. I had put my aluminium plate under my feet to keep them away from the dampness of the floor. A black dung beetle climbed on to the plate to crawl over my leg, and I struck it off with my foot.

My *munaqqaba* cellmates rose habitually in time for the dawn prayers, whereupon I would hide my paper under the tiling in the corner of the toilet . . .

Those eyes are looking straight at me through the slits of the *niqaab*. Boduur and Fawqiyya say she's a spy, working for the Internal Security police. Her eyes, though, are innocent, childish. Her name is Itidaal.

She approached me – in the manner of a child – and asked, 'What are you writing?'

'A story.'

Her eyes shone. 'A love story?'

I laughed. 'Yes.'

A delighted smile. 'I wish I could read it. I've been engaged to my cousin for three months now, and I started wearing this *niqaab* one month ago, for his sake. He reads the Qur'an, but I don't know how to read anything. I never went to school. I'd like to learn how to read – all the girls here except me can read. Can I learn?'

'Of course. You're still very young. How old are you, Itidaal?'

'Sixteen. How many days will it take for me to learn to read?' she asked anxiously, eagerly.

'Sixteen. One day for each year.'

Her laugh was childish too. Long and unbroken, like a whinny. 'Will you teach me?'

'I don't mind.'

She gave me a hug, hopping up and down in delight. Happiness, like infection, spreads rapidly. I felt that I, too, had become a child, my heart filled with pleasure. The pains in my back disappeared, and my body felt strong and energetic. I went to the steel-barred door: the dawn breeze massaged my face with invigorating moisture. The sky was still black, but the early light was creeping in slowly.

Suddenly, I heard the voice of the curlew. My heart beat forcefully, and I jumped on to the bars, clambering up them with my bare feet, stretching my neck skyward, jamming my head between the two steel bars.

I can't see him. The voice, though, affects me as if it's me that he's calling. A sweet, sad voice, piercing the silence. A lone flute in the darkness. Singing like a mother's voice, like offering a prayer of supplication, like weeping, like a child's abrupt, long laugh, or like a single scream in the night. Or an uneven sobbing which goes on and on.

Every dawn, I wait for that voice, and I hear it. Every dusk, too. the curlew sings only in the stillness and the dark. Only in this moment which falls between night and day. A single bird in the universe. . . I raise my head toward the sky. I want to see him. Never in my life have I seen a curlew. The sky, though, is surrounded by walls and wires, and in prison we hear the curlew without seeing him. That's enough, to hear him without seeing him. Enough that I see a drop of dawn light, and a drop of dew. Enough that my fingers can take hold of my pen. I still have paper, too, over which the pen can move. It's not important for me to see the words. Nothing matters except the birth of words on paper, the dawn's birth, the gloom dissolving . . .

I put on my sports shoes in preparation for my morning exercises. Moving the body means life, and bodily strength means strength of mind and soul. In prison, one needs all of one's forces.

Behind me, I heard the sound of bare feet jumping up and down, hitting the ground. It was Itidaal, who had finished her dawn prayers, removed her *niqaab* and cloak and begun to do exercises.

The sweat poured down, washing away my sleeplessness and fatigue. All my back and neck pains dwindled away. Exposing my body to the shower's spray, only now did I feel wonderfully refreshed, revived as if I had just been born, at this very moment. My appetite was ready for a new day. I was very hungry, and insanely thirsty for a cup of tea.

That morning, Fathiyya-the-Murderess showed up carrying a hoe, which she handed to me. 'Plant the enclosure, doctor. I planted our enclosure, the one in the murderesses' cell, and the place became like a paradise. I planted *mulukhiyya* greens, watercress, parsley, *ful*-beans . . . roses and other flowers.' She tapped the ground with a strong heel. 'The ground here is all stony. Knock out the stones with the tip of the hoe. The earth in this area, around the Barrages, is rich. Dig way down, and you'll get to the really good black soil.'

The feel of the hoe in my hand and the movement of my forearms rising and falling gave me a sense of pleasure. I'd strike the ground with all my strength until sweat was pouring from my body. An enjoyment akin to intoxication took over my body and mind.

I've not held a hoe since I was a child. My brother and I used to compete with each other for it. Although he was bigger than me, and his legs were longer, I used to beat him to the hoe. I love this rigorous movement which works all the muscles of the body. I love the smell of the earth's underside when I cleave it, and place the seeds in the clefts. The water running in the long channels carries the aroma of silt, of vast green fields, of green crops lustrous under the sun.

During every summer holiday, we used to travel to our village, Kafr Tahla. In happy anticipation, my brothers and I would hop about excitedly, dreaming all night long of the fields, of riding donkeys and of the aroma of freshly baked country bread and pancakes. We would dream of my grandmother and aunts – my father's sisters – smothering us in kisses, of my aunts' daughters, earthenware jars on their heads, letting us accompany them to the Nile to fill the jars and to fish.

We also went to my grandfather's house in Cairo every summer holiday. It was a palatial villa, surrounded by a large garden. I recall a big dog which barked constantly, and I remember my maternal aunt with her sharp, high-pitched voice, screaming whenever she saw me walking on the fancy embroidered Persian carpet in my dirty shoes, and taking a towel to the brass doorknobs and everything else which I touched or on which I stepped. I detested this aunt, my mother's sister, and I hated the palace with its carpets and gleaming doorknobs. I loved my father's sister, the peasant woman, and I recall with fondness the mat on the floor on which I could walk while wearing shoes, on which I could lie down . . . I could even roll in the dirt and no one would scream. I'd take hold of the doors which had no shining knobs, and no one would follow me with a polishing cloth. I'd leap on to the donkey and ride into the field, or it would carry me along the edge of the canal, breaking into a run and still I wouldn't topple off.

The handle of the hoe is of rough, twisted wood; my hand curls around it with all the strength I have. The stones in the ground break apart only after vigorous, hard blows. Stones of red and white.

I raised the hoe above my head, bringing it down on the rocky ground until the stones were in pieces. The blood flowed from my hand. I tied it up with my white handkerchief and went on digging. Energy stored since childhood welled out from somewhere deep inside me, and I felt a tremendous pleasure at being totally involved in something, absorbed as I was in extracting the rocks from the ground.

How many hours of that day passed as I worked with the hoe? I don't know. But I was oblivious to time, as one hour followed another. I forgot that I was in prison.

I stopped at the sound of a voice. I saw Latifa looking at my flushed, sweat-drenched face and the white handkerchief, wet with fresh, red blood, which wrapped my hand. I heard her say, 'That's enough. Tomorrow you can get on with the rest of the enclosure. Your hand is bleeding.'

I answered her with childish stubbornness. 'I have to finish it before four o'clock today, before the *shawisha* locks us into the cell.'

A few minutes before the hour of four, I'd finished digging up the entire enclosure, which now looked like a tiny ploughed field. Dhuba collected the red and white rocks outside the enclosure, forming a large, high pile. Exhausted, I threw myself on to the ground, my chest heaving. The handkerchief around my head was filthy with blood and dirt. Latifa gazed at me for a long time, her eyes bewildered. 'I didn't realise until today what a tyrannical demon there is inside you.'

I leant my tired back against the wall. 'I didn't feel at all relaxed until today. The imprisoned demon has finally got out.'

That night, the pains returned to my back and chest. Beneath me I could feel the wooden board extended over the broken slats, although it was below the thin, blackened rubber mattress. Massaging my neck, I had to extend my fingers to scratch my head. Something small was crawling on my skull. I tried to take hold of it before it could flee into the roots of my hair or creep down the opening of my *gallabiyya* to fall on to my back.

During the first few days, I had not shut my eyes at all. From the very first day, I'd been liberated from the geckos, cockroaches and mice – everything except those little creatures which bite the skin of the head or crawl during the night below one's underclothes to disappear between folds of skin. Many nights passed before I could free myself of these as well – but then my presence triumphed over theirs and I became capable of sleeping as if they were not there.

I couldn't sleep deeply at all, though. On that bed, I could never get my backbone into a straight position. Some part of my body would always sink between the slats, nearly touching the floor. Sleeping on the ground would have been preferable if it had not been for those creatures who crawled by night from the enclosure into the cell. Small animals and insects entering through the bars . . . chirping, whistling, squeaking, biting, overturning tins and plates.

When I told the *shawisha* that I could sleep only on a straight wooden board, she left the cell and was gone for a while. When she returned, she was breathing heavily, and Dhuba was in tow carrying a wooden board. The *shawisha* had come across it in a storehouse in the prison, and she presented it to me as a gift.

The board was long and narrow, and it shook with my slightest movement. I couldn't turn over without waking, and I had to get up in order to change my position on the board. If I turned over while fast asleep, I'd find myself on the floor. But after a few nights, my body began to toss about freely and yet I did not wake or fall off. I'd open my eyes in the morning and find myself lying stiffly like one crucified, a circus performer atop a wire, or an Indian fakir sleeping on nails. I'd regard my body in wonder the likes of which I'd never felt before, at its extraordinary ability to adapt and to sleep profoundly under the worst of conditions.

In prison, night is longer than day, but daytime is more repulsive than the night, for the darkness conceals the blackened cracks, the garbage in the corners, the fingerprints and spatters of blood dotting the mattresses, walls, steel bars, bed posts, waterpipes, toilet doors and water spigots.

In our quarters there were three ancient brass water spigots. One tap had been stripped off, the second yielded not a single drop of water, and the third gave off a constant gurgle, day and night. In the corner were three toilets, one of which was blocked up and could not be used. The second had neither a door nor a flush. The third had a flush which did not work, and half a broken door which would not close tightly, while from the shower installed in its ceiling dribbled an unending trickle of droplets. Whenever any of us used the toilet, she would feel the water dripping on to her head from the shower, while her feet would be plunged into the overflow of sewage from the toilet opening, and around her the large cockroaches would go darting about.

Invariably, when Boduur entered the toilet, we would see her bounding out before she had finished her business, yelling 'Cockroach!' No sooner would we hear her shout than we would run towards her, each of us grasping a shoe in one hand, swordlike, ready to strike the cockroach down.

One day, we heard Boduur's scream as she sat in our enclosure. We assumed that a cockroach had attacked her, so we stripped off our slippers and prepared ourselves for battle. But instead of a cockroach, we saw a man. Boduur was not wearing her *niqaab*, and the idea that a man might see her face and hair uncovered terrified her. She leapt from the enclosure into the cell in one stride, to hide her hair and face under the veil.

After that, whenever we heard Boduur yell, we paused before removing our slippers to ask: 'Cockroach or man?'

One time, to prevent a man from seeing her head bared, Boduur stumbled on the threshold to the cell and fell on her face while running inside, breaking a front tooth and wounding her upper lip. But the blood pouring from her mouth did not stop her from running to conceal her hair beneath her *niqaab*.

On days when the heat was truly oppressive, Boduur would sit beside the other *munaqqabas* as they sat in the enclosure, all without their usual outer cloaks and *niqaabs*. Each one held a copy of the Qur'an in her lap, her glance half-fixed on the page and half on the outer prison courtyard. No sooner would one of them catch a glimpse of a man's shadow in the distance than all would jump to their feet, springing into the cell to don their *niqaabs*, outer cloaks, and gloves.

In the prostitutes' cell which faced us across the big courtyard, the very same explosion of movements would take place, but in the reverse direction. Running out of the cell, the inmates would uncover their long hair, as they tossed winks in the men's direction, laughed, and popped bubbles of chewing gum.

In the women's prison, a man – any man, even an elderly convict coming in to collect the garbage – became a figure of consequence, one who would generate a major commotion among the veiled women on the one hand and among the imprisoned prostitutes on the other. I used to observe these men, with their smiling faces, cocky in their new-found importance as each one noticed the tremors caused by his passage among the women and girls, whether the latter were distancing themselves or emerging and drawing near.

When the men concerned were the prison's administrators, however, the prostitutes did not react in their usual fashion by revealing themselves and approaching. Maybe in their opinion these weren't men, or perhaps police garb had stripped its wearers of their essential maleness. Perhaps the authority derived from power – or the fear of that authority and power – sweeps away human feelings and sensations, including instinctual drives, as it advances.

Dhuba's eyes filled with anger and shame when she saw her sister prisoners, those from the prostitutes' cell, rushing to crowd around a man. Her voice carried a sharp edge as she called out, 'For shame, you prostitutes!'

In response, one of the prostitutes would twist her lower body in a suggestive manner, place her hands on her hips, and yell across, 'Shut up, you beggar, you sham prostitute!' She'd run into the open courtyard, her buttocks moving visibly inside tight jeans. Dhuba would hurl a mud brick at her while screaming back, 'I'm not begging over here in the political prisoners' cell, I take my fair share through hard work. These are women to respect, these political women – so there, you thieves and sham prostitutes, you!'

Giving her middle a shake, the woman across the way would yell back. 'You sweep out the cell over there for the price of a cigarette, you beggar! I'm a prostitute, a good and proper one, and no one here can call me a thief!'

A thin woman with frizzy hair and a face bearing the traces of wounds slapped the speaker across her rear, exclaiming in a loud voice, 'What's wrong with thieves, anyway, and where do they come in? I sweat for my fair share, and I don't sell my honour, either, you dope addict, you drug pusher you!'

A light-skinned, corpulent woman jumped to her feet and shouted, 'Shut up, you, I pray God your tongue falls off! What've you got against drugs? I buy and sell hash with my own money and on my honour, but I don't steal, you thief, you daughter of thieves!'

They began to trade insults, one grabbing the other's hair, as arms and legs became interlocked in a fight which was ended only by the *shawisha*'s bamboo stick.

The eyes of *Shawisha* Nabawiyya were tiny, and her inflamed eyelids were bare of lashes. Yet her eyes held an unusual power of observation, and her nose, too, must have been particularly sensitive. The black hairs emerging from her nostrils trembled like the whiskers of a cat or a rabbit whenever she drew near to the spot where we buried forbidden items. These started with pen and paper, expanded to include newspapers and finally a transistor radio the size of a cigarette packet. We buried all of these things together in a hole in the ground. At closing time, after the *shawisha* had locked the cell door upon us, we would extract the newspapers, reading them one after another and then burning them in the toilet before the *shawisha* would come to unlock the door at eight o'clock in the morning.

She'd enter sniffing the odour of burnt paper. Her small eyes would take in the charcoal-like slivers, black as soot, as they spilled across the surface of the sewer water overflowing from the round hole ringed by cockroaches. Her eyes would meet ours; she would say nothing. The matter was no secret, for nothing in prison is really off limits as long as one knows exactly how to proceed.

Thus, we came to follow the news, within Egypt and across the world. During the first few days, we learnt nothing. We began to glean the news from the lips of the prisoners strolling in the courtyard, and when Dhuba – or whoever was substituting for her – came in each morning carrying our loaves of bread, we asked her the news. Indeed, even before asking, we could sense from the look in her eyes and the tone of her voice whether the news had improved or got worse. The same was possible with *Shawisha* Nabawiyya – or whoever was taking her place. Despite the small, half-closed eyes which were capable of displaying the opposite of what she harboured inside, we were able to plumb her depths, unravel the riddles and codes therein, and interpret the movement of her head, the look in her eyes, the way in which she would open the outer door to our area each morning, her hand as it pushed open the steel door to the cell, her head as she peeked in from the door, her voice saying 'Good morning, ladies', her manner of sitting in the enclosure, her disappearance from the enclosure, her return with a quickened step, and the particular way that the two immense keys in her grip swung.

To a prisoner, the senses are akin to the nerves of perception for a blind person – the nerves of smell, touch and hearing – for which extraordinary new capabilities are generated.

We came to know the exact hour at which a search would take place, before it happened, and the moment in which the Internal Security police officer would show up, before he arrived. Our latent senses developed skill at picking up any unusual movement in the expanse of courtyard, and the *shawisha*'s face became like an open book in which we could read as we pleased.

By night, we gathered around the small radio, bringing our heads close to the broadcaster's mouth. His voice was faint, the batteries were weak. Suddenly, Sadat's voice would ring out; the radio would grow louder. As if it were a cataract, the voice surged. His breathing was choppy, and ours followed suit.

Our future hangs upon these breaths, and on these words that shoot out like torpedoes.

Suddenly, his breaths were cut short; his voice went completely silent. One of the *munaqqabas* jumped up delightedly. 'He's talked so much, he's run out of words and dropped dead!' Our hearts pounded and our eyes took on a sparkle. But someone else commented, 'It's the battery that's died. We've got to buy a new one.'

Our solemnity and despair returned. Buying a battery for the radio was a problem. It was impossible to purchase batteries from the prison canteen, as we purchased cigarettes, but buying them from the market outside required money, and we had none. Each of us offered something in payment for the battery. One gave a leather handbag, and another presented a pair of shoes. I gave a piece of my clothing. And we got a used battery.

Sadat's speeches were long – a single speech could consume an entire battery. Whenever his voice was cut off suddenly we would think that he'd had a heart failure and our own hearts would begin beating faster. Soon enough, though, we would discover that it was the battery which had run out.

The radio was more important to us than the newspapers, for we could move the dial and listen to broadcasts from all over the world. News of the internments in Egypt was being dispatched worldwide: Sadat had put those who opposed him into the prisons, and still he was talking about democracy. Even the announcer for Voice of America was saying that democracy in Egypt was not genuine.

I could see the eyes around me flashing. Through a *niqaab*, a pair of eyes shone as a delirious voice emerged: 'The whole world is with us, and against Sadat!' Another voice was saying: 'Our news has reached everywhere – they're attaching great importance to us.'

The joy of the prisoner at not being alone! The whole world follows one's news behind bars. The whole world voices opposition and protest.

The small radio – the size of one's palm – was like a strange magic object, which could transmit life, merriment and optimism. Hearing a sympathetic news item, we would break immediately into enthusiastic applause. The newspapers, however, were just the opposite. We were only able to obtain the Egyptian newspapers, which were all against us in their repetition of the speeches in which Sadat had accused us of instigating the sectarian rift and conspiring against the nation. They slapped the charges upon us without any trial, and passed judgement on us without running any investigation – while we were in prison, unable to make any response or to defend ourselves.

From the 12 September 1981 issue of *Al Ahram* newspaper, page eight, I clipped a cutting of several lines.

I will preserve this clipping for the time that I leave here to go to the investigation session. I will confront the investigator with what the newspapers have written about us prior to any investigation.

The clipping stated the following:

Consultative Council Discusses Decision Arising From President Sadat's Speech

The Executive Committee of the Consultative Council has confirmed that the Presidential decree concerning the precautionary detention of certain individuals has not been aimed in the slightest at the political opposition but rather at those conspiring against the interests of the people. This is indicated by the fact that the loudest voices in the opposition, who have attacked the ruling system with the greatest vehemence, both within the country and abroad, were not included in the precautionary detention order. They are completely at liberty, enjoying freedom and democracy in the era of Sadat, the Great Hero, and under the protection of a state based on institutions and the law.

How can the Consultative Council press charges of conspiracy against us without running an investigation?

I placed the clipping in our subterranean hiding place.

I'll take it with me to the investigation session. If there is an investigation.

Every day, we awaited the summons which would call one of us to depart for investigation. But one day followed another without any departures or investigations. At night, unrolling the blanket across the floor, by the door, we sat together, each of us trying to imagine the questions which the investigator would ask her.

If the charges were trumped up, then the questions would have to be fabricated as well. We tried to compose the questions which might be contrived for any one of us, and we came up with the answers as well.

'If the Socialist Prosecutor asks me why I eat twice a day instead of three times,' one cellmate asked, 'how should I answer?'

Someone was ready with a reply. 'If he asks you that question, ask him "Why did they name you the Socialist Prosecutor?"'

'They called him the Socialist Prosecutor so there would be something socialist in this country,' remarked a third.

'Nothing left of socialism except the Socialist Prosecutor,' commented another.

'They called him the Prosecutor so he could prosecute us with lies and slander our names.'

'I dreamed yesterday,' one of the younger cellmates said, 'that I was seated before the Socialist Prosecutor. He said to me, "You're charged with attempting to overthrow the ruling system." I asked him, "Was I really all that the ruling system needed? It's already turned head-over-heels without me."'

'Every night I dream of the Socialist Prosecutor,' said another. 'And every morning, I put *kohl* on my eyes so I'll be ready to go out and meet him. He's become the only man in my life.'

Laughter rang out through the cell. Everything around us seemed comical – the prison, the steel bars, the taut police-like faces. The convulsive voice on the radio. The slogans in the newspapers. The picture on the front page every morning. The mouth open to its widest, the heavy breathing, a fist waving in the air, the words mixed with foamy spittle. The peculiar accusations. Statements from the Interior Ministry, the Consultative Council, the Office of the Chief Prosecutor, and the Socialist Prosecutor.

Are we living a farce? A girl aged sixteen, totally unaware of political matters, is charged with overthrowing the state.

When our laughter rings in the night, the sharp screeches of the cockroaches are cut short. They put out their feelers as they scamper into the corners, and they stand motionless for a moment as if to listen intently. One of our group claps her hand over her mouth to suppress her laughter, saying, 'Don't laugh out loud, the Internal Security policeman is making his rounds in the cells, plastering his ear against the wall and listening to us.' Another chuckles. 'Poor chap! Tiring himself out for nothing.'

'We're not attacking the state,' replies someone else. 'To the contrary, we've all fallen in love with the Socialist Prosecutor and we've started dreaming about him every night and putting on eye make-up for him every morning.'

'He might be coming in right now to search the cell!' shrieks another as she springs to her feet.

'It's a search, folks – hide everything we're not meant to have.'

'Hide the radio, the gas burner, and the newspapers.'

'The eyebrow pencil! and the toilet paper.'

'And whoever's been overturning the state had better put it right again!' Their laughter and their voices ring in my ears like those of secondary school students. Their eyes sparkle like those of my schoolmates, years ago, in Helwan Boarding School, when we used to poke our heads out from beneath the covers after the bell had announced bedtime and the dormitory light had been put out. We'd whisper and laugh together, two to a bed, or three, or four. No sooner did we hear the footfall of the Matron in the outer corridor than each girl scurried to her own bed, drawing in her head under the covers and closing her eyes, straining her ears for the sound of those crepe-soled shoes as the mistress entered on tiptoe to spy on our forms, search through our dreams, scrutinise the workings of our minds as we slept, and count us one by one, making certain that each of us had gone to sleep in her own bed and that our chests were rising and falling regularly beneath the covers. If it seemed to her that the chest movement was irregular, she used to pull off the bedclothes to make sure the eyes were closed in genuine sleep. If she noticed an eyelid fluttering, she yanked the girl out of her bed by her forearm and propelled her to the disciplinary chamber.

If she stripped off the bedcovers to discover four eyes instead of two, she rang the warning bell, rousing all the dormitories. Everyone would awaken to hear the scandal: Mistress Nazira has uncovered a crime in the making! She's caught two girls sleeping in one bed!

I was a child of twelve and I had no idea what the crime was. I heard from the older students, though, that sexual fantasies filled the head of Mistress Nazira all night long, giving her insomnia and causing strain. In a state of nervousness, she'd get out of bed and make the rounds of the dorms, unable to calm down until after she'd seized a girl or two, and had given them a good hiding.

The first time that my eyes fell upon Shukriyya, the prison warder, I thought immediately of Nazira, the boarding school mistress. The same tall, thin body. . . stooped back. . . long head, looking pointed at the back. . . short, coarse hair. . . facial muscles contracted dejectedly. Nervousness and tension. Bulging eyes darting here and there, shifting about herself like the eyes of a surrounded animal. A long nose, hooked and sharply aquiline, like the beak of a kite. Lips so thin they'd practically disappeared. A triangular chin, pointed and hooked. Arms, shoulders, back, buttocks, thighs – all crooked and bowed.

When Nazira was silent, we couldn't tell whether she had a mouth, for we could see only a deep line stretched beneath her nose as if it were pulled by wires. When she talked, though, her face was cleft suddenly by a broad, round, toothless hole.

As a little girl, I used to believe that her teeth had fallen out because of the tension showing on her face and the constant clenching of her jaws as if she were consuming her teeth and tongue. I believed my older schoolmates when they said that once she had eaten a piece of her tongue. Once, out of curiosity, I tried to peer into her mouth, but she was taller than I, and her mouth was higher than my shoulder.

In prison, however, I noticed that my shoulders were higher than Officer Shukriyya's – and I could look into her mouth. I saw that she had sharp yellow teeth, like those of one addicted to smoking or narcotics.

I felt sympathy for her. I hoped she would open her heart to me and tell me the tragedy of her life. As she was searching through my handbag one day, I asked her, 'Why did you start working as a prison warder? Do you enjoy opening other people's handbags?'

She clamped together her lips in anger.

'You can be sure that I'm not against you,' I said. 'I know without any doubt that you are not my enemy. You and I have the same enemy.'

My words scared her. What frightened her more, though, was seeing me jumping up and down in the enclosure, in my sports shoes and the knee-length athletic shorts which my husband had sent to me with my other sports garb in a small suitcase. She was a firm believer in the shamefulness of women's knees, especially in prison. Unlike Boduur, however, she believed that it was God that would reckon with me in the hereafter and that she could not overstep the sphere of God's authority.

What really scared her was that the contagion of athletic exercise spread through the bars to the prisoners in the courtyard. As soon as they saw me hopping up and down in our enclosure, they would stand in front of me in a long row and jump like me. When I raised my arms high, their arms went up. When I clapped my hands together above my head, their hands clapped. When I bent my torso, they folded their torsos. When I raised my head high, their heads went up. When I jumped into the air, they jumped. If I stamped the ground with my feet, they did the same. If I called out 'one, two' they shouted with me. 'One, two!'

The prisoners knew the time at which I usually exercised. At nine o'clock every morning, they gathered in front of the door to our enclosure in their long white *gallabiyyas* and bare feet, standing ready. No sooner had I begun than they would form themselves into a row to start, staying with me, movement by movement.

Warden Shukriyya would appear in the courtyard at the sound of hundreds of hands clapping in unison. The din scared her; quivering on her thin aluminium heels, she shouted, 'Everyone into her own cell, quickly now!'

No one left the line. I han't finished my exercises yet, and I resumed my movements, as the row of prisoners followed me without a pause.

The warden stamped her feet on the ground in anger. She approached me and said to me through the bars: 'This is a provocation to revolt inside the prison!' 'The prison statutes,' I replied, 'do not prohibit physical exercise.'

I didn't stop exercising, and neither did the row of prisoners. Every morning at nine o'clock precisely, I saw them standing there, waiting, smiling, bodies stretched, ready.

One day I was slightly late, and their voices called out to me. 'Doctor, it's nine o'clock! Doctor!'

I ran towards them breathing hard, as if trying to make an appointment on time. I began my exercises. I moved my legs and arms in that regular rhythmic movement which resembles dancing. Before me I saw a long line of arms and legs, moving through the air, striking the ground with the same, regular rhythm.

As if my body and theirs are one. As if there are no bars or steel partitions between us. As if we are one body.

I was aware of my heart beating beneath my ribs and I could feel the sweat pouring down my face and into my mouth, the sharp bite of its touch pleasing to my tongue. In my head, I could still hear the echo of the voice and the words it had uttered: 'This is a provocation to revolt inside the prison!' I could sense my brain cells opening to embrace a truth as if I were comprehending it, in fact, for the first time. Any organised group movement, even if it be merely bodily exercise or dancing, establishes a rhythm in the mind and body which resembles the pattern of revolution or revolt.

It was as if Warden Shukriyya had discovered the concealed workings of my brain cells before I had. And Mistress Nazira, the boarding school mistress, had been exactly like her. She had unlocked the hidden talismans of my mind as I slept, seen my dreams before I did, and understood the movements of my body before my own mind had grasped them.

Yet it is nothing but a dream, a delusion. And soon indeed the taut, exercised bodies would disperse or go lax, or run off in alarm at the sight of the cane with the pointed head. I would find myself standing alone behind the bars, staring into empty space, sports shoes still on my feet. I might resume my movements alone, but they would seem meaningless to me. I would turn around to enter the cell, but then I would catch sight of the hoe and I'd hurry over to it with new hope.

Lifting it high with all my strength, I brought it down to strike the ground. The earth revealed its black, fertile belly and I evened it out with my palm. I felt its pulse. It was warm beneath my hands, warm like my arms and legs. Its aroma was like mine, the scent of silt and sweat falling in droplets from my body. I strewed seeds all around me, and covered them with ash as I covered my body. I ran to fill the bucket and water the ground until its thirst was satisfied.

Fawqiyya heard me requesting Fathiyya-the-Murderess to bring grape and orange seeds. She groaned. 'Will we still be here when the soil brings forth grape vines and orange trees?' I was taken aback by the question. Perhaps I'd forgotten that I was in prison, or maybe while sowing seeds, I didn't consider the harvest. Often, I write without thinking of publication. Writing in itself is pleasurable, and so is planting. Work is inherently a source of pleasure. 'Whether we remain here or not,' I said, 'what's important is that I'm planting.'

'Planting without a yield is no pleasure,' she said. 'It's meaningless.'

'For me, planting is an aim in itself, and it *is* enjoyable. Anyway, what do you mean by "yield"?'

'Will we stay here until we're eating grapes and oranges from these seeds?'

'If we stay, we'll eat them,' I replied. 'If not, whoever comes here after us will eat them.'

She pressed her lips together, turned on her heel and entered the cell. But her taut lips remained before my eyes as I lifted my arms, bearing the hoe, over my head, my eyes raised to the sky, ready to lower the hoe to break the earth apart. But my arms remained high in the air for a moment, and my eyes to the sky. It seemed to me, as I brought down the hoe, that I was breaking not the earth but time.

I want to kill time to free myself of the burden. The burden of waiting. . . of wary anticipation, of sharpening my ears every day, every hour and every minute for that voice calling my name.

I would start to believe that I was not waiting, that I had been born here and would die in the same place, and that I was occupied constantly with other matters. No sooner would the *shawisha* open the door to the cell than I would run out to the enclosure to dry the clothes I'd washed, and to dry out my mattress and blanket under the sun. I would circle the enclosure fifty times before starting my exercises. After the exercises would come gardening, then the group sessions. . . discussions – lectures – analysis of the latest news – preparation for the interrogation sessions – monitoring conversations between the *shawisha* and Dhuba or Fathiyya-the-

Murderess. . . By night, tutoring Itidaal in reading and writing, then seating myself on the base of the jerry can and writing.

I welcomed the act of writing with avidity and desire, forgetting that I was in prison, waiting. But as soon as I moved my head in the direction of the high barred window, I realised that I had not forgotten, and that deep inside me was a long wait – a frightening wait, like that of anticipating death. I hid the expectation, this awareness of waiting, from myself, from my accessible intellect and my inner mind. It was an anticipation which I did not recognise or want to avow.

It was not the anticipation of interrogation or of the session before the Socialist Prosecutor which I sensed, but rather that of the final exit. . . the everlasting one. . . release!

Anticipating release. This was something I had killed off since the beginning, since the first moment I'd entered prison. Nothing kills a human being as waiting does.

In prison, one does not die of hunger, or from the heat or the cold, or from beatings or sicknesses or insects. One might die of waiting, though. Waiting transforms time to timelessness, the tangible object to nothingness, and meaning into meaninglessness.

I opened my eyes on my first morning in prison and found that I was not anticipating anything: not a departure for investigation, or release, or visits from the family. I'd forgotten I had a family or a home or another life outside this place.

The greatest attribute of human beings is that we forget. Would I have survived in prison without the ability to forget?

The eyes of my child, as he opens them in the morning and does not find me or know where I am. . . On that particular morning, had he opened his eyes? How long ago? I did not know. . . perhaps it had been a century. . . for time, in prison, is something other than time as we know it, and a single hour extends before us endlessly, like a lifetime or like eternity.

I stare into the darkness. Dawn has not yet broken. I am rolled up like a foetus in its mother's belly. I can sense the warmth coming from the walls which surround me. Have I died and returned to the original womb of my birth, or have I not yet been born?

Total silence and the darkness wrap me like a black cloak. An icy thickness presses on my ears in a continuous, unending whistle. I extend my head out between the bars, and I watch the first drop of light appear. The first dewdrop. An intense thirst burns my throat. What did I have for supper last night? I don't recall. I don't remember anything. I've even forgotten my child's features.

The sad, sweet voice cuts through the silence. The lone flute in the darkness. A call like a mother's voice, like a prayer of supplication, like weeping, like the long laugh of a child or a solitary scream in the night.

Every dawn I wait for him, and I hear him. I raise my head towards the piece of sky visible through the bars. I can't see the curlew. I'm satisfied just to hear him without seeing him. Enough that I hear, and that I can move my arms and legs, and jump up and down on the floor of the cell, that my heart beats, the sweat pours, my body goes under the shower and the thick water falls. . . and that I dry my hair, and light the gas to make tea.

We kept the gas burner hidden inside a cardboard carton beneath one of the broken bedframes. Around it, we placed our tins of sugar and tea, *ful*-beans and lentils and treacle. Beside these items we kept our clothes, in cardboard cartons, suitcases, or paper sacks.

At first, the cats used to come in by night through the bars on the door. They overturned the tins of molasses on to our clothes, and tipped the tins of sugar on to the tea and both on to the lentils. We lodged a complaint with the prison administration and they placed wire on the door which would no longer permit the cats – or other animals the size of cats – to enter. However, smaller creatures, insects, and bugs could still come in.

I found the gas burner dificult to light – as did everyone in the cell. It was the sort with a wick; the gas must fill the container to a certain level, and a certain length of wick must show. If we pulled the upper end of the wick a few millimetres too far, the flame leapt into our faces, burning the ends of our hair. If we pulled on the lower end of the wick just a few millimetres more than necessary, the burner would not work at all, or the gas would flame inside the container and fill the cell with smoke. Then, at a run, we distanced ourselves from the gas burner, fearing that it would blow up in our faces. We would try to extinguish it. However, it required quite an operation to extinguish the burner – a process more difficult than lighting it. Four or five of us had to encircle it, blowing on it continuously until it went out, leaving behind a cloud of thick, black smoke and a stifling odour of burnt gas.

Every time we lit the burner, I asked myself what we would do if a fire were to break out in the cell. After four o'clock in the afternoon, the *shawisha* always locked us inside the double steel doors and went home. All of the prison's administrative personnel went home at that time too. Only the woman who kept night watch remained. She was called *sahharat al-layl*, 'nighthawk'.

Every evening we heard the call resounding from one of the cells: 'Hey, *sahharat al-layl*!' It was a call which might continue all night, sounding like an extended scream, an ever-present wailing, like begging for mercy or a despairing supplication in a darkened sky whose mute, blank uniformity does not respond. A goddess without ears. Like the siren of the ambulance – but the doctors are asleep and so are the guards. No one hears the voice of the supplicating woman except a few women who surround her, calling in one breath: 'Ahh, *sahharat al-layl*!. . . a woman is dying.'

This woman dies: no one comes to the rescue. The women around her cover the corpse with a blanket, weeping in stifled voices, and then they fall asleep. In the morning, the women of the cells go out behind her, wailing loudly, screaming and slapping their cheeks, mourning for her and for themselves.

The wailing pierces through the bars to reach us as we sit on the ground in the enclosure, picking through *ful*-beans or lentils to clean them, our backs resting against the wall. Eyes meet – dull, worried, exhausted eyes. Like those of caged animals, they await the day of slaughter or the day of death. Her hands encased in black gloves, one of the *munaqqabas* clutches her head, wrapped in blackness, and prostrates herself, head to the ground, whispering 'God's mercy upon her.'

'O Lord,' respond the *munaqqabas* in unison.

Another clasps her head in her hands and bursts out crying. A third *munaqqaba* smiles. 'Faith in God, friends. Nothing happens except through God's will.'

Still another: 'She's resting now, from the pains of the world. God has shown mercy, look, for she has been released.'

'She's got release without Sadat's permission!' laughs another.

'God's permission is above Sadat's. God is greatest.'

In unison, they call out: 'God is greatest.'

In the night, the call sounds again: 'Ahh, *sahharat al-layl*.' Perhaps it is another sick and dying woman. Or it is a woman giving birth, and the plea is mixed with shrieking and crying. In the end, silence takes over. End of the night, before the threads of dawn creep in. . . the curlew's voice breaks the silence, like that long plea, or a long, uneven sigh. On the heels of the curlew's call comes the sound of the call to prayer. A woman performs the ritual invitation to the dawn prayer, and all of the *munaqqabas* arise to pray. They carry out their ablutions with water from the pail, or from the jerry can if the water has been cut off. They don cloaks and gloves, and stand in rows behind the woman prayer leader, to begin the communal prayer, to offer supplications and further prayers, and to repeat the names of God. They press their foreheads to the ground and call in one voice, 'God is greatest.'

In prison, three colours reign: white, black and grey. Three tones which create the impression of illness, demise and death. And illness in prison is worse than death, for it is a sort of long, slow death, or it is to experience death hundreds of items rather than just once.

From the very first moment in which I saw the prison doctor and his clinic, I decided not to get sick.

Does one become sick by one's will? Yes, and sometimes no, except that a person may be able to will herself or himself to get sick and even to die. The opposite is also true – one might will oneself not to become ill or to die.

On the morning of the day after I entered the prison, they took me for a medical examination in the clinic. This is an obligatory prison procedure for all new prisoners, or rather for 'the new imports'. This includes a medical examination of the heart, chest, abdomen and extremities; height and weight; notating any distinguishing marks on face, head or body. A picture is taken of the prisoner, standing, her back to the wall, a brass plate on her chest bearing her number and fingerprints. The picture is placed – together with fingerprints, descriptions of the head and body and height and weight measurements – in a dossier in the medical clinic, while copies are put into another dossier in the administrative offices of the prison and into still another in the Ministry of the Interior.

The female warden and *shawisha* took me to the clinic, which is in that filthy building that they call the hospital. On the way to the doctor's examination room, I passed the tuberculosis ward, the scabies ward, and the ward for other infectious diseases. The gaunt, emaciated faces and feeble, withered bodies were stretched out on the ground. I noticed the blood-infested spittle, the odour of rot, and the white bandages blackened by dust, pus, and blood.

Before the door to the clinic stood queues of new prisoners, standing in wait for their medical examination: thin bodies in white *gallabiyyas*, standing in rows, clinging together, worn out. Yellow-ish faces, eyes without focus, irregular breathing.

I remembered my years, long ago, in the Qasr el-Aini Hospital in Cairo – a major hospital run by the Ministry of Higher Education – and in the free hospitals run by the Ministry of Health. I remembered the same queues, the same faces, the same pale gauntness. Even the same curses that I recalled were escaping now from the mouths of the prison clinic's doctor, the female doctor's aide, and the two male nurses.

One difference, though: in those hospitals, the patients are in a better state than they are here. There, after a long wait, they return to their homes carrying a bottle of medication. It might be a blend of rhubarb and soda, or any other mixture. . . black or white in colour. . . it will not cure their illness, and it might give them another, but in the end they return to their homes and families.

But here, there's no return to home or family. 'Here' means a long wait, night and day, summer and winter, without any return, without a home, without family. 'Here' means simply swearwords, for the cursing ends only in kicks and disciplinary cells. 'Here' means illness. No cures, no medicine except pills with no name or colour which the nurse wraps, with her blackened fingers, in a bit of soiled paper – toilet paper or old newspapers – or sometimes she doesn't wrap them at all, merely tossing them into the prisoner's hands or into her lap.

In spite of that, leaving the cell to go out to the hospital was a lovely dream, hardly attainable. The hospital was no more than forty metres from our cell, but this meant forty metres through the spacious prison courtyard. And we were prohibited from going out to the courtyard or even walking one metre length in it.

Whenever one of my cellmates became ill, she informed the *shawisha*, who went to inform the warden, who went to inform the *ma'mur* (the senior prison official). The *ma'mur* informed the Internal Security officer.

If the Internal Security officer thought that the matter called for a doctor's examination, he ordered the prison physician to go to the political women's cell. The doctor might come right away, or he might appear after finishing his work – depending on his circumstances.

The first time he entered the cell, I did not know that he was a physician. Moreover, I did not realise that he had been one of my contemporaries in the College of Medicine. His features appeared unfamiliar, as if I were seeing him for the first time. His demeanour resembled that of a policeman, and he wore police uniform too. It was the first time I had seen a doctor in the clothes of a policeman.

Do clothes change one's features? Perhaps it is the position itself, or the life in prison in the company of the police, which shapes an individual's identity and appearance and gives similar features to the colleagues of one profession.

However, as soon as he began to speak, and to walk before me in the cell, I remembered him. He had been my colleague in the College of Medicine about 25 years before. He had a distinctive voice, nasal and quite harsh. He ended every sentence with a gasp. When he walked, he moved one arm forward while the other remained stiff, held closely against his body. He was tall, thin and light-complexioned, wore spectacles, and carried a briefcase always stuffed with books. He used to place it on his knees when sitting in the lecture hall. I recall his head bent over the notebook and the pen in his hand, moving quickly, faster than the professor's lips were moving. If a single word passed him by, he used to raise his head from the paper, bewildered eyes starting out of his head, his lips sagging, turning to look around like a drowning man seeking rescue.

He reserved the same seat every day, claiming it with his briefcase before the lecture was to start. The first seat in the first row, on the far right, next to the aisle near the door. No sooner did the lecture end than he would jump up from his seat, into the aisle, and from the aisle to the door, to scamper into the College courtyard and enter the operating room or the laboratory or the other lecture halls in order to reserve the first seat in the first row next to the door.

His briefcase never left him. In the lecture hall, it was on his knees if a male colleague was sitting next to him, or – if a female colleague sat beside him – he placed the case between himself and her. In the operating room or laboratory, the case rested between his legs or on the floor between his feet.

He used to memorise the lectures word by word, as if they were the Qur'an. Whenever a classmate asked him at what time a certain lecture would be given, he replied: 'If God wills, it will be on such-and-such a day, such-and-such an hour, by God's permission.' Whatever he said, he began it with the phrase 'If God wills' and ended it with the statement 'By God's permission'. One day, a colleague asked him, 'What time is it, Sabir?' He replied, 'If God wills, it is one o'clock.' Ever since that day, his colleagues had called him 'Sabir If God Wills.'

They caught him one day in flagrante delicto, committing the crime of sitting in the back of the hall. For the first time, his briefcase was not at his side; rather, next to him sat a female colleague, without any intervening space or partition. The College began talking of the strange story of his love, and of that woman classmate who had made him leave his seat in the first row. They began talking of his Christian faith as well, for he announced his conversion to Christianity and married her.

I said, in astonishment and that delight which accompanies a chance meeting with an old classmate, 'You are Sabir Barsum!' I saw his features contract into a frown, so that his face took on a policeman-like look, and he said self-importantly, 'I'm Doctor Sabir Barsum.'

That day, one of the *munaqqabas* was ill. She was determined that he would examine her without removing her cloak or *niqaab*. He tried to convince her that he could not examine her unless she uncovered her chest and abdomen, but she refused adamantly. He turned towards me. 'Try to persuade her, Nawal.'

'My name is Doctor Nawal, not Nawal.'

I had felt sympathy for him when he was a student. Now, I found his situation despicable. From the prisoners, I'd heard many anecdotes about him, and the *shawisha* had told me some things as well. How can a prison doctor become a police tool for oppression, pain, and mutilation? When he uses medical science and surgery for revenge or punishment. When he accepts money for granting a sick leave or not granting it. When the prison doctor becomes more dangerous than the executioner! For the latter beats and tortures only, but the doctor can amputate an arm or a leg. He can pluck out an eye. He can deform the mind with poisonous pills. He can do anything to a prisoner, woman or man, without being discovered by anyone.

We'd heard many stories of this sort about him. We used to see him strolling through the prison courtyard, flirting with the prostitutes, using offensive language. All the cellmates agreed to throw him out if he came into our cell. To the *ma'mur*, they said: 'We have a doctor in the cell. Why can't you give her the necessary medical instruments instead of having the likes of this prison doctor come to us?'

I told the *ma'mur*: 'I'm prepared to practise my profession as a doctor among my cellmates in the cell and for the other women prisoners in other cells, especially at night when the prison doctor sleeps.' But the prison administration refused. For I was in prison as a prisoner, not as a doctor. In prison, among the losses a prisoner sustains is the loss of profession. Since one loses one's humanity, personhood, freedom and name, why not one's craft as well?

One day, two of my cellmates were stricken by scabies. I recognised the disease immediately and demanded that they be treated and isolated from the rest of the inmates so the illness would not spread. A young doctor whom we had never seen before came to us, confirmed my diagnosis, and wrote them a prescription for treating scabies. But they were not put into isolation, and all the inmates in the cell began to scratch themselves.

We did not know what had happened. We heard strange rumours to the effect that some of the senior officials in the prison had directed the blame on the young doctor. How could he announce to us that the illness was scabies? He should have rejected my diagnosis or lied to us, by saying that it was merely an ordinary skin irritation, or mosquito bites, or bedbugs, or anything else, as long as it wasn't scabies. What would happen when the news seeped outside and everyone knew that the prison was contaminated with scabies and infectious diseases? The medical reports which Dr Sabir Barsum had written said that the prison was clean and that there were no sicknesses or infectious diseases within.

The young doctor disappeared from view. We heard that he had been transferred from the prison to some other place. Dr Sabir Barsum came to us in anger. He looked at the fingers of the two sick women and said in a peeved voice: 'Who said this is scabies? That isn't so, it's just an ordinary skin rash!'

I drew near to him and looked straight into his bulging eyes. I fixed my eyes on his and said, 'I am a doctor. I know this is scabies and nothing but scabies. Moreover, a young doctor who has since disappeared corroborated my diagnosis and we don't know what happened to him. You may be afraid of the Interior Ministry or the prison administration, but we are not, and we will not keep quiet about this situation. Our health is threatened, and you are the prison doctor. You should be caring for our health, not deceiving us. This behaviour of yours contradicts the oath which you swore in front of the Physicians' Syndicate. You are transgressing the law of the Physicians' Syndicate, and that of the profession of medicine and the law of humanity.'

One of the *munaqqabas* shouted, 'You are not a doctor! You are an executioner!'

Another called out, 'Don't you know what the prisoners say about you? Don't you know what your reputation really is in this prison?'

They called him 'Sabir Barsum With A Cigarette.' At first, we did not understand the meaning of this name, but *Shawisha* Nabawiyya explained it to us: 'He can write any medical report. He has no conscience. Our Lord spare us his evil! Any small compensation, or a cigarette, and he'll sign for a sick leave.'

Sabir Barsum came to dread approaching the vicinity of our cell. If one of our cellmates notified the authorities that she was ill, another doctor would be sent to us. One day, we saw him entering the cell and we managed to expel him collectively, in one go. I saw him running outside the cell, seeking the nurse's arm as shelter. Sabir Barsum lodged a complaint against us with the prison administration. All of us spoke against him. The Internal Security police officer asked my opinion and I replied, 'We have no confidence in him. It would be preferable to send a different doctor to us or not to send any doctors at all.'

And we no longer saw Sabir Barsum. I ran into him once after I'd got out of prison; he lowered his head and vanished.

Sitting on the ground of the dirt enclosure, my fingers encircling a pointed sliver of mudbrick, I inscribe the letters of my name on the ground. I contemplate the shape of the letters, and I study myself. Who am I? Prisoner No. 1536. They have stripped me of everything, even my name. But I remain myself, and I prefer to be 'the prisoner' inside this prison than 'the prison doctor' – Dr Sabir Barsum or any other doctor.

Ever since I'd entered the College of Medicine, I'd felt alienated from those men with bulging eyes, distended briefcases, swollen eyelids and reddened eyes, who spend all night memorising lectures word for word, and step on others' toes in order to reserve seats in front rows, gasping for breath as they run from the lecture hall to the operating room, clutching a scalpel in one hand and a sandwich in the other. They cut short their meal breaks and limit their hours of sleep. They have no concern but memorisation and nothing before their eyes but the spectre of the examination. And no sooner does the examination end than the memorised information begins to seep from their memories. . . and they become doctors. . . in the University, in the Ministry of Health, in the Interior Ministry, and in the prisons. . . and in the private clinics. They look at the invalid's pocket before diagnosing his illness, stack one pound on top of another in the drawer of their desk in the clinic, and then die of heart failure. No one remembers them, for they leave nothing of value behind. Their children or wives inherit a few buildings or shops, or large expanses of arable land. But no one remembers them, not even their children and wives. The families become occupied with their large inheritances or with the project of a new marriage.

Ever since I'd become a doctor, I'd felt alienated in the company of this sort of doctor. They are like shop owners, selling good health and medical treatment to invalids who don't even have the price of food. A doctor of this sort jams a fat black cigar between his teeth and turns up his nose at one as he speaks, like a god – even though some of the time his diagnosis is wrong. The invalid may die, or he may be rescued, depending on his own condition. And whether he lives or dies, he must pay, whether in advance or in arrears.

What sort of profession is this? Can this profession possibly be my profession? Can I place one pound on top of another in the drawer of my desk in the clinic, then die of heart failure, leaving nothing valuable behind? Am I to live and die and leave nothing for my children, and for those who come after me, but a large patch of soil whose ownership they contend?

Since childhood, I've wanted to live my life and to die leaving behind me something of value. What, though?

A question which I turn over in my mind. My fingers sift through the dirt. Its touch on my hand reminds me of my childhood . . . in our village . . . I used to love playing in the dirt. Pouring water on to the ground, I'd transform the dirt into fresh clay from which I moulded a person's head. Making two holes to resemble my grandmother's eyes, I'd look into them and laugh with the other children. We buried the head in the ground and watered it, and when we returned to it the next morning, why, there would be a green stalk growing out of each eye.

My grandmother's eyes were the hue of the plants. She inherited her eye colour from her father the Gazan, who had emigrated from Gaza to Kafr Tahla and married off his daughter to a young peasant called 'Hibish', named after his own father who had emigrated from Ethiopia to Egypt while still in his mother's womb.

My grandmother was very tall and slim, with a head held aloft and a bearing which intimated a primitive, rural sense of pride. Not a single man or woman in the village pleased her, not even her husband. He was feeble and perennially ill, always urinating blood; he died while still a young man. She did not weep for him. She wrapped her head in a black kerchief and swore that her son would not be a peasant. She sold her silver anklet (her marriage dowry), bound her stomach with a wide sash to keep herself from eating, and gathered her pennies, one by one. She collected the price of a train ticket plus enough to cover school expenses, and sent her only son to Cairo to get educated. Her six daughters stayed with her in the hamlet and married poor peasants who tended the earth with their hands and urinated blood.

When her son would return at the summer break with a diploma and certificate of excellence, she would ask him: 'What did you come out? What's your place in the class?' 'Second,' he would tell her. She would call out, slapping her palm down, 'Why aren't you first? Is the top student better than you? Didn't he come out of a belly just like this belly of mine?'

My grandmother used to recount this anecdote to me, striking her stomach with the palm of her hand and laughing. Actually, that happened only once, and afterwards your father always took first place.'

I drew my fingers from the soil and looked up: a head resembling my grandmother's, wound in a black kerchief. The features, though, are different, and so is the voice. So is the time.

Time becomes confused for me here. I don't know if I am the child playing in the dirt or the woman caged inside the prison. My childhood and adolescence, and all the stages of my life, seem to be intermeshed into one period of time, or it is as if there is no such thing as chronological time.

I study my fingers, unrolling them before me in space. They look as my fingers did when I was a child, and the dirt is like that in which I used to play. The same odour, colour, and feel on my hand. And the water . . . I pour out the water, and the dirt becomes a muddy paste. I fill my palm with water from the little canal, or from the irrigation channel.

One day, I took off my clothes and waded into the channel to swim with the other children. Then, like them, I began to release blood with my urine.

My mother noticed the reddish urine and shrieked in alarm: 'Bilharzia!' My grandmother laughed, saying, 'It's not "harsa" at all! Red urine is the sign of good health and strength. All peasants have red urine.'

I went to the doctor, and he gave me twelve shots straight into the jugular vein. The red hue vanished and the old pale yellow colour returned to my urine.

I lifted my head from the ground and saw the face of Gamal Abdel Nasser – his bronzed, dark complexion, his piercing, gleaming eyes – sitting on the wide raised platform during the National Conference for the Popular Forces in 1962, flanked to his right and left by grave, tense faces, held taut as if stretched by wires. A voice rang out in the air asking, 'Who is the peasant?'

An apprehensive silence prevailed. Thought, contemplation, analysis. They scratched their heads. They brought in dictionaries and reference books. The sweat poured from their faces as if they were sitting a tough examination. Then they began to answer, competing with each other as though they were pupils. They all spoke at the same time, interrupting each other, attacking one another, accusing others of not knowing the correct answer or not understanding the question.

What is the question?

The question is repeated. Who is the peasant? The contest begins anew. They vie to arrive at the definition that is correct – or the definition that is desired. They collide with each other, pushing one another off with hands and forearms, stamping on others' feet to reach the front seats. They raise their voices sharply, enunciating their words with exaggerated precision. Donning spectacles, they scrutinise books and reference works, making the rounds of bookstores and going to the National Library in Bab al-Khalq. They compete in forming committees for research and study. Sitting, smoking, crossing one leg over the other and enquiring: What exactly is wanted?

The question is repeated yet again: Who is the peasant? The competition begins – let the vicious circle spin once again.

I was sitting in the vast hall, observing them. Some had removed their suits and put on peasant *gallabiyyas*. Their soft fingers bore no resemblance to the fingers of those who grasp hoes. Their lips were rosy, and between them jiggled luxury brand cigarettes. Their Arabic diction was invaded now and then by foreign-language terminology.

My turn came to speak. They directed the question at me. Who is the peasant?

'The peasant is the one whose urine is red,' I replied.

Silence fell. An indignant silence, as the faces grew troubled for a moment, and then the heads turned in my direction. I was sitting in one of the back rows. . . an unknown young woman without position, title, prominent family or clique.

They took note of my old shoes, the heels eaten away. They realised that I did not own an automobile, or have the taxi fare, or possess enough money to buy a new pair of shoes.

On a slip of paper, three words were fixed with a Parker pen next to my three names: Uncalled-for boldness.

Since then, the name has been on the black list and inside a yellow file in the Interior Ministry.

The *shawisha* lifted her small eyes, and I saw that they were covered by a white cloud with the translucency of tears. She was sitting on the blanket in the dirt enclosure as was her custom. But she was unusually quiet, her face paler and more lifeless than I had ever seen it. When Fathiyya-the-Murderess came in with the tray, the *shawisha* did not extend her hand towards the food.

'What's wrong with you, *shawisha*?' called out Fathiyya-the-Murderess.

It was as if she had been waiting for the question: the imprisoned tears poured out. She wiped them away with the sleeve of her scabby grey overcoat and spoke.

'All night I was awake by my sick boy's side. The doctor came and said my son would have to have an operation to remove his right kidney. The doctor demanded fifty pounds before the operation and fifty to be paid after it.'

'Fifty, fifty – so what?' commented Fathiyya-the-Murderess. 'Money can go to hell.'

'What's expensive becomes cheap for the boy's sake,' said Dhuba.

'The money is there, praise be to God,' replied the *shawisha*. 'Money isn't the problem. It's the operation. I'm frightened of the operation. It's a difficult one.'

The *shawisha* turned to me. 'What do you think, doctor?'

'It is not a difficult operation,' I said. 'But has the doctor examined the other kidney?'

Her face grew even paler, as if the blood had disappeared completely from it. Her voice had become feeble. 'The other kidney is not in good shape. . . that's the awful part.' She wiped her sleeves across her tears. 'The doctor said we'd gone too long without seeing about treatment. But the boy was fine! His urine has always been red, all his life – I didn't know it was blood. Do you think he'll die, doctor? Isn't there any hope?'

'There's always hope, because any part, any small part, of the kidney can work to compensate for the rest,' I explained.

'Our Lord give you peace, doctor. Day and night, I've been thinking . . . he's my son, my only son, and since his father's death he's helped me scrounge to find enough income to support his sisters.'

'Leave things to God and don't think about them, Nabawiyya,' said Fathiyya. 'Thinking destroys the heart.'

Dhuba sighed. 'In our situation, one has to forget that she has a heart.'

'But the only son is dear!' exclaimed Fathiyya.

'What is dear becomes cheap in prison,' said Dhuba with a toss of her hand.

'Shut up, Dhuba, shut your mouth,' called out Fathiyya angrily. 'What is dear remains dear, and what is cheap stays cheap. To a mother, her only child is dear, dearer than her own life. I killed for the sake of my daughter Haniyya. I came to prison, to spend the rest of my life here, for her sake. For her good, I threw myself into total ruin. I live for her – I go to sleep and wake up with the single hope that I'll get out and see her, and hug her close to my chest. If it weren't for her I would have died on the very day I came into prison.'

'What did she gain?' asked Dhuba. 'Her father's been murdered and you, her mother, you're in prison, and she's alone now without anyone to raise her.'

Fathiyya hung her head and remained silent, despondent. Her eyes stared blankly, lost, sorrowful. Then she spoke in a faint whisper as if only her ears were meant to hear. 'True. . . what has she gained? Nothing. She lost her mother and her father in a single day. But I wasn't thinking about her when I killed him. I was thinking . . . I was thinking . . . about what? I don't know. Maybe I wasn't thinking? My mind stopped working from the shock of seeing him on top of her.'

Fawqiyya had come out of the cell and seated herself in the enclosure next to Fathiyya. She spoke in her usual forceful voice, pronouncing her words emphatically as if she were giving a speech or explaining a scientific fact of which she was absolutely certain: 'It's psychological shock, no doubt about it, caused by the emotional nature of a woman, and by a wife's jealousy toward her husband when she sees him in this situation! You were jealous, no doubt!'

'I am not like the rest of you, women of the town!' shouted Fathiyya-the-Murderess. 'I never felt any of this jealousy business toward my husband. It was I who went looking for another wife for him, one who would give him a son, and help me with the housework and field chores. If I'd seen him with any woman I wouldn't have killed him – but with my daughter! My daughter is my treasure, a piece of my own heart and soul, but my husband . . . A husband, no matter how much a stranger . . .'

One of the headcovered women called out in astonishment, 'Your husband was a stranger?' Fathiyya-the-Murderess gave her a dismissive wave. 'Of course he was a stranger. Not of my flesh or of my blood! But my daughter is my own flesh and blood.'

Dhuba laughed in genuine pleasure. 'By the Prophet, you've got it right, Mama Fathiyya. All my life I've felt that my husband was a stranger to me. . . if it weren't for the marriage papers! But what are we to do? God willed marriage for us. . . and God willed prison for us.'

'It's all according to God's will,' replied Fathiyya-the-Murderess. 'Even murder.'

'I ask God's forgiveness!' called out one of the *munaqqaba* women. 'Our Lord did not tell you to kill . . . so ask God to forgive you. Say "I repent and ask your forgiveness, O Lord." Feel some regret for your crime.'

Fathiyya made an angry gesture. 'Regret? Never! Impossible for me to feel any regret about it! By God, if I saw him in front of me now I'd kill him again.'

The *shawisha* laughed. 'After all, she's a murderess at heart, and daughter of a murderess too.'

Fawqiyya spoke in a preacher-like voice. 'If you hadn't murdered, you'd be outside the prison at this moment, with your young daughter who needs your care and training. Wouldn't it be better to bring up your daughter than to enter prison?'

Fathiyya jumped to her feet. 'And you, Madame Fawqiyya?! Wouldn't it be better for you to bring up your children instead of coming to prison? At least I came here for the sake of my daughter . . . and you? Why did you come to prison?'

Blood rushed to Fawqiyya's face and she spoke in a tone of anger. 'You entered prison for a reason which concerned you alone, an egotistical reason, an individualistic one—but I came in for the sake of the nation and those who are poor!'

'And your children?' asked Dhuba. 'Who brings them up and watches out for them?'

Fawqiyya was shouting. 'Our Lord watches over them! Our Lord is present.' She went on with hardly a break. 'Our Lord is present, but children are a problem for any mother who wants to serve the nation. She is torn between her duty toward her children and her duty to her nation. In my opinion, the national duty comes before any other.'

From inside the cell, Boduur called out. 'The religious obligation to God and the Messenger[1] comes before all other duties. God before the nation!'

'Open the door for me, Nabawiyya,' said Fathiyya-the-Murderess. 'I have work to do. I am a peasant woman and I don't know anything about this sort of talk. I killed . . . and I've admitted that I killed. I killed my husband for the sake of myself, in order to save myself from living with a man who was oppressing me. He wronged me all my life, and I served him like a slave serves a master. He never in his life said one pleasant word to me. My life with him was black from the first day to the last. Every day, I'd think, "I'll kill him", until I saw him with my daughter Haniyya. A person can't kill easily, or in a single day or night. The whole time I lived with him I thought about killing him. Open the door for me, Nabawiyya, I've got things to do.'

The *shawisha* tossed the keys in her direction, saying, 'Mur-

---

[1]Messenger: *Al-Rusuul,* epithet for the Prophet Muhammad, founder of the Islamic faith and first leader of the Muslim *umma* (community). This epithet reflects Muhammad's role as transmitter of the Qur'an from Allah to the *umma.*

deress, daughter of a murderess. Fathiyya, everyone who's come into prison has felt regret except you.' Fathiyya laughed, snatching the keys as they hit her lap. 'Why should I feel any regret? My life in prison is better than my life was with that man. What's wrong with prison? It's for men who are strong and plucky – and for the pluckiest and strongest women!' She let out a loud, ringing laugh as she opened the door and burst through to the prison courtyard.

Her steps are firm and strong. Her head is high and her bearing proud as she walks, her features and movements resembling those of my paternal aunt's daughter.

Natural and basic as the earth, with the earth's solidity. Her voice is clear and strong, as direct and firmly unequivocal as a knife edge. Her eyes shine, and her laugh reverberates through the dirt enclosure.

I look at her strong brown fingers, and it occurs to me that they resemble my fingers. My heart beats as if with the same force which powers her heart. My eyes shine with the very same lightning sparkle. My hand, as it grips the pen, is like her hand when she took hold of the hoe and struck the blow.

It is just as if I were striking blows with the pen at a corrupt, black head which wanted to abduct my freedom and life, to deform my true self, and to force me to sell my mind and to say yes when I want to say no.

Over the ground, my fingers sketch letters and interlacing circles. My hand trembles with anger, and my heartbeat quickens. If my fingers had not come to know the pen, perhaps they would have known the hoe. The pen is the most valuable thing in my life. My words on paper are more valuable to me than my life itself. More valuable than my children, more than my husband, more than my freedom.

I prefer my place in prison to writing something which has not originated in my mind. The sincere word demands a courage akin to that needed to kill – and perhaps more.

My fingers chisel the letters in the dirt. I contemplate the words which are circling round in my head. What appeared to me as certain a moment ago I see now as surrounded in the fog of doubt.

To this moment, I don't know why I am in prison. I have seen no investigator or prosecuting attorney or lawyer. I heard the *shawisha* say that she heard they were saying I entered prison because of my writings. . . my crime, therefore, comes under the rubric of crimes of opinion.

Is free opinion a crime? Then let prison be my only refuge and my final fate!

But does free opinion really merit the hardship of prison? The fatigue and hunger and illness and the harsh life in this tomb-like cell? My father, my mother, and my acquaintances – all of them – believed that I would be the cleverest of physicians and the greatest of writers. . . that I was created for success, and for arriving at the top. It would have been possible; I could have been like that – I could have obtained the highest position and title, lived in a veritable palace, owned a yacht, and married a prince or a great ruler.

But since childhood I have abhorred rulers and authority – ever since I saw my mother rebel against my father when he raised his voice against her, and ever since I heard my father cursing the king, the government, and the British.

I was a child; my mother imagined that I did not see her rebellion, and my father thought that I did not understand what he was saying, or that I would forget as I grew older. . . but I did not forget.

My mother taught me how to write when I was a young child. She grasped my hand in her own and wrote letter after letter. The letters of my name, sketched in front of me in the ground of the enclosure, look as if they are inscribed in my childhood handwriting. My name, then the names of my father and paternal grandfather – the official triple name which I wrote out for the very first time on my school notebook. I was a child and the name sounded strange – especially as it included that of my paternal grandfather. Why should the name of this stranger who died before I was born be part of my name?

I scratched out his name with my pen and wrote my mother's name next to mine. Then came the names of my father . . . sister . . . brother. The teacher came along and scratched out all the names written next to mine. She left only the name of my father and that of the stranger whom I had never seen in my life.

Since childhood, I've detested having the name of my grandfather attached permanently to my name. I loved my mother, though, and I loved her name, Zaynab. No sooner had the teacher turned her back on me than I rubbed out the name of my grandfather again and wrote in my mother's name.

My fingers move over the ground, wiping out the name. Bitter-tasting phlegm in my throat. Nothing to eat since yesterday. The cockroach lying on the plate. Thirst, hunger . . . and in my imagination a set of objects comes to light: a clean plate, a piece of grilled meat, red tomatoes . . . and – next to the plate – a cup of pure, clean iced water!

I move my tongue in my throat and swallow the bitterness. I move my head towards the door of the cell and catch a glimpse of my bed: the wooden board suspended between the two bedframe posts. How am I able to sleep all night on this board without falling off?

In the back of my head floats a whitish, fog-like object. It's a clean, white sheet, stretched over my bed, in my own bedroom. The face of my husband. . . the face of my daughter. . . of my son. . .

Without delay the light was cut off and the image vanished.

My heart is heavy, and the bitter phlegm accumulates inside. My stomach is utterly empty; I can feel it under my hand, like a growth. Seems my hand can almost pierce through to my backbone. A deep pain, like an old wound, throbs beneath my palm.

Now I feel doubts about everything. What is the use of writing? Dead words, dying on paper. And for whom am I writing? And who reads? Was even a single voice raised when I went to prison?

A sarcastic laugh rang out, and a harsh, caustic voice coming from afar reverberated: 'We are in an underdeveloped country ruled by a single individual like the one god of monotheism. If you obey him, you get to the top, and if you rebel against him, you get buried in the ground!'

I recognised the voice: one of my male colleagues, a writer. He had arrived at the top and was sitting there on the summit. One day I asked him, 'How can you tell me one opinion and write another?' He laughed sardonically and asked, 'Don't you believe what is said about democracy?'

'Whether I believe or not,' I replied, 'I write my own views and the results don't concern me.'

'I'm concerned about the results,' he said. 'I don't want to lose my position – I want to raise my children well and send them to the finest schools.'

His voice is still in my ears – with another voice, that of my aunt, my mother's sister. She did not educate her daughter, but married her to a landowner. Her voice is sharp, ringing in my ears as it did when I was a child: 'A woman's place is home, husband, and children. Why do you put on airs? Are you a man?' Other voices, many others, are ringing in my ears, as if coming from the pit of the earth. My body feels cold and heavy as if it is a corpse buried deep in the earth. A cloud hovers over my eyes. The darkness around me is thick, and I can barely see. But I notice a feeble light in the distance, a quick gleam. Two star-like eyes and a voice resembling that of my mother. In fact, it *is* my mother's voice, and her eyes are looking into mine: 'If my father had not married me off, I would have gone on with my education. I used to love reading and writing, I wanted to do something important in my life – not just give birth to children like a litter of cats.'

Her eyes blaze like torches. Her body is light and briskly active. Her gay laughter rings out in the house, long and broken like a child's moaning and sweet like the voice of the curlew, singing in the morning upon awakening and in the evening before sleeping. She married my father at the age of 17, and had my nine siblings and me over the space of nearly 30 years, and then died when she was 45. Died clutching my hand in hers, her perplexed eyes fixed on mine in a childlike bewilderment.

It was a knifing pain in the small triangle beneath the heart and just above the abdomen, an old and chronic chest pain from the time that my mother seized my hand, her eyes widening in bewilderment, and died without giving me her name. She gave me life, and she has given me the revolution ever since I was a child. But a strange man married my grandmother and died before I was born, affixing his name upon my existence.

She wanted to read and write and change the world, but her day was spent in the kitchen, feeding nine children and their father. She went to sleep only to awaken pregnant with the tenth child.

She jumped from the balcony to abort it, and it died, leaving the taste of bitterness within and a chest pain in her right breast.

She placed her hand over the pain and said to me, 'It's right here – the pain is stabbing me like a needle.' My hand froze against her breast, and was paralyzed momentarily. Her eyes widened in childlike amazement and she asked, 'What have you found?'

My throat was dry, and my eyes shifted to avoid hers. 'Nothing at all! It's just a pocket of fatty tissue.'

She believed me at once. She always believed me. She had trained me during my childhood to tell the truth, and here I was, lying to her for the first time . . . and to my father, and to all my brothers and sisters.

I concealed the secret somewhere within me, in the deep folds of my heart. The secret kept me awake day and night, shredding my guts, knifelike.

But let the knife remain in my heart . . . I won't pull it out and plunge it onto her heart . . . or theirs.

I can see her laughing, her laughter merry like that of a child. In the morning she sings . . . she doesn't know that death crouches in her chest, ready to pounce . . . eating the cells of her breast . . . moving from the breast cells to those of the lungs as quickly as the blood can circle from her chest to her heart.

Medical science had no remedy for it. Medicine failed, science failed, and the Medical School professors were powerless even to lessen the pain. She would certainly die immersed in pain.

No sooner did the pain disappear momentarily than her face began to shine and she smiled like a child. She believed, with the child's naïvety, that the pain had gone, no more to return, and that she would rise from her bed and walk to the bathroom . . . and that she would sing every morning.

One moment, or one smile, would light her face with hope. Then the pain would return to consume her body, day and night. She would clutch my hand in hers and squeeze it, or she would grasp the hand of my father, or the hand of one of my sisters or brothers, or the bed post, and squeeze, moaning in a suppressed voice, bearing the pain in anticipation of the next moment of hope.

She didn't know that it was death – that there was neither life nor hope for her. I did not want to keep her from having a glimpse of hope, from the one smile which could lighten her face for a fleeting moment.

Nor did I want to prevent my father, brothers, and sisters from the boon of hope and the expectation of her recovery.

I carried the truth like a mountain: it was heavy like a mountain. I bore it myself; seeing their eyes full of hope, I fled far away from them. When no one was looking, I cried soundlessly so that no one could hear my sobbing.

She continued to moan in her weak, enervated voice: 'Death is more merciful than this pain . . .' her wide eyes interlocked in mine, seeking help from me through the days, the nights, the months – 20 months.

I filled the syringe with painkillers, a bit more every time. I brought the needle near to her arm. Her eyes were on mine. My fingers trembling, I plunged the needle into the vein and thrust the liquid into her blood.

A new thought occurred to me: perhaps there is hope after all! Who knows? Perhaps she will recover. Perhaps all those doctors were wrong. My confidence in doctors and medicine was minimal. My confidence in my mother was greater. Perhaps her will would triumph over the illness and she would get well!

Suddenly my fingers stiffened, and my hand became paralysed. The syringe fell on to the ground before all the liquid had gone into her body.

I moved my head in her direction. I did not see her eyes. I did not hear her voice. No part of her moved. I threw myself down beside her, whispering in her ear: 'Mama!' I went on whispering but she did not answer. I glanced around in alarm. I was afraid to leave the room. I was afraid that my father or one of my siblings would come in. Perhaps they would see the crime in my eyes! My heartbeat was audible, and my voice as I called out might have aroused suspicion. I was imploring her to awaken, not to die, to save me . . .

My father entered the room, and so did my brothers and sisters. They called out in alarm. 'What's happened?'

Before I could confess the crime to them, my mother opened her eyes suddenly, just as she used to do at the sound of me, calling to her, when I was a child. Indeed, she used to open her eyes even before she could hear my voice, when she simply understood that I was calling her. Awakening from a deep sleep, she would go from her bed to mine to make certain that I was all right or to cover me.

After that day, she lived 30 more. It seemed to me that she stayed alive through that period just to protect me . . . to deny the accusation . . . to make certain that I understood she was dying on her own, and to lift from my heart a burden or a sense of regret which might kill me.

I raised my eyes from the ground. The eyes of the Internal Security officer were regarding me suspiciously. 'What are you writing?' He stared at the ground for a long time. He understood nothing. Letters and circles intertwined and superimposed.

He remained standing before me for a long while, examining the ground of the dirt enclosure. He saw the slim green stems emerging from the earth, and he noticed the hoe, propped in the far corner next to the high wall. In panic, he roared, 'Where did that hoe come from?'

He issued orders immediately to the *shawisha*, and the hoe disappeared in the twinkling of an eye. 'Gardening is not prohibited,' I explained to him. 'All the prisoners plant things.'

'The hoe is off limits,' he said. 'All sharp implements are forbidden.'

He remained standing on the threshold between the cell and the enclosure. I was seated on the ground. Inside sat my cellmates, some on the ground and others on the beds. All were looking at him with eyes that were silently threatening and furious. The whites of their eyes were stained with the yellowishness of carbon dioxide poisoning and the smoke of burnt gas, while the corners were red, inflamed by sleeplessness, worry, and flies. Dry lips, pale skin infused with red and blue lines, the result of continually scratching at one's skin. Clothes soiled by the dust, *gallabiyya* collars blackened.

He remained there, standing, staring at us with eyes we could not see behind his dark glasses: a pale-skinned face, a clear complexion imbued with the redness of blood, and the glasses. He had drunk milk and fruit juice before coming in, and he'd had a hot bath. His collar was clean and white, showing no trace of sweat or dirt. His muscles were relaxed and loose. He'd slept soundly on a soft bed through the night. A cellmate shrieked: 'Only animals could live in this cell!' Another added, 'No . . . animals would refuse to live here . . . they'd get angry, they'd rebel . . . they'd kick . . .'

The Internal Security officer smiled and spoke in a calm voice. 'My apologies, ladies, if I have caused you any annoyance. But it was not me who issued the order to imprison you here. I am only a civil servant who carries out orders.'

I recalled the voice of my eminent writer colleague: 'I am only a civil servant . . .' The writer is a civil servant . . . the thinker is a civil servant . . . the philosopher is a civil servant . . . thus, we have no writers, thinkers, or philosophers. What is the difference between the Internal Security officer who is a civil servant and the writer who is a civil servant? Both carry out orders. Neither wants to lose the monthly salary, or the position.

I stretched my neck and raised my head, my eyes towards the sky . . . my mind, free, soaring upwards . . . I think as I wish, and I write – with my fingers, on the ground – what I wish to write . . . No one threatens me with dismissal from my job, since I have no job. No one threatens me with prison, since I am in prison itself. No one can threaten me with death, because the life we are living here is indistinguishable from death.

My chest filled with air, my heart with blood, and I heard my heartbeats, pulsing strong and free. I prefer my place here on the ground, in the dust, to that of the Internal Security officer on his elevated threshold bound by the fetters of his position, or to the place of my colleague the great writer, sitting on the pinnacle of literary achievement with a frightened heart in his chest and a salary in his pocket which – however it might grow – remains meagre beside the loss of his free opinion.

The Internal Security officer still stands on the threshold between the enclosure and the cell. The eyes which gaze at him are red and angry as he repeats, 'I am only the one who carries out orders, and I am waiting for new orders to come from above.'

'From above?' Itidaal called out. 'From where, above?'

He smiled. 'From Our Lord.'

'No, not from Our Lord,' she shouted. 'Our Lord does not imprison innocent people.'

'Who said you're innocent?'

'I don't know anything,' she said in a loud voice. 'Not even how to read and write!'

'Why do you cover your face with a veil?' he asked.

'Because God has commanded me to do so in his Noble Book.'

'How did you find that out? Have you read God's Book?'

She was silent for a moment. 'I don't read, but I heard it on the radio over at the neighbours . . . and I heard the Shaykh say that God has commanded all women to cover their faces.'

Itidaal had told her story before. Boduur had not believed her, and Fawqiyya, too, had expressed misgivings. I was sitting in front of Itidaal, observing her eyes as she related her story. They were the eyes of a child of sixteen, and her voice, too, was that of a child.

'I don't know how to read or write because I've never been inside a school in my life. My father divorced my mother when I was a child. I don't remember what my father looked like. I've heard about him from people. They've told me he's been married ten times. He was forty years older than my mother. He divorced her and married a girl younger than me. My mother is thirty – she has married again and is with her husband in Upper Egypt. I was all by myself in Cairo, living with my grandmother – my mother's mother. She's only fifty years old, but she's blind and never leaves the house. Two months ago, I wasn't putting on the *niqaab*. I used to go out in the street wearing an ordinary *gallabiyya*, nothing covering my hair. One day, when I was sitting at my neighbours' place listening to the radio, I heard a Shaykh saying that a Muslim woman must wear a *higaab* or else she'll be damned eternally to hellfire in the afterlife. My cousin – my mother's sister's son – confirmed the Shaykh's words and told me, "Itidaal, the *niqaab* will protect you from the fire." So I began wearing a *niqaab*. On Friday, I went out to visit my aunt. As I was passing by a mosque, I saw four men carrying rifles. They surrounded me and said to me, "Get in the car." I asked them, "Where are you taking me?" I saw a police officer with them; he asked me, "Where were you headed?" "To my aunt's," I told him. He said, "I'll take you to your aunt." So I got into the car and they brought me here.'

Boduur's loud voice was sceptical. 'Did you really believe him when he told you he'd take you to your aunt?'

'By God Almighty, I believed him. As God is great, I am telling the truth. Why don't you believe me?'

Boduur did not believe her, nor did Fawqiyya. Her black eyes were filling with tears, and she approached me. 'Do you believe me?'

I looked her in the eye. 'Yes.'

She had only a single *gallabiyya* during the whole time we were in prison. No one from her family asked about her or sent her any clothes. She used to clutch at the door bars, as she sat alone, crying.

One night, I awoke to a faint, moaning voice. She was asleep, tears on her face. A child's face. Like the features of my daughter, as she sleeps. Her long hair was tumbling over the edge of the bed, and the cover had slipped from over her body.

I got up and covered her. She opened her eyes and whispered, 'As God is great, I am not lying!' I patted her on the head. 'We all believe you. Don't cry now, try to get some sleep.' She waved a thin hand in the direction of Boduur. 'Why does she doubt me?' I saw Boduur's face as she lay sleeping in her own bed – that deep vertical line on her forehead, a scowl which clung to her even while asleep. In the facing bed I saw Fawqiyya, sleeping too, on her forehead a frown which had taken the shape of a deep horizontal line.

This frown was constantly in place, day and night. It grew deeper as we opened our eyes to a new day. All of us would exchange smiles, and customary greetings – 'Good morning!' – except Boduur and Fawqiyya, who were constantly frowning and scowling, their lips always pressed together tightly. If a merry laugh were to ring out in the cell, the scowl would widen and the frown would grow deeper.

For Boduur, we learned, laughter was a shameful act, one which was against the religious law. As for Fawqiyya, she used to press her lips together in affected gravity and say, enunciating her words with exaggerated emphasis, 'What is the use of laughing?'

'Laughter,' I replied to her, 'is similar to athletic games or dancing: it strengthens the heart and chest muscles and vitalises the brain cells. Laughter is centred in the right section of the brain. If the cells of this spot grow ill or lazy, one becomes incapable of laughter. Laughing is a sign of thinking and evidence of the active quality of the mind. Laughter helps to propel the adrenalin into one's blood, and quickens circulation of the blood to the cells of the brain and heart. Laughter does not signify licentiousness, or a lack of restraint – just as scowling does not indicate seriousness!'

Fawqiyya was incapable of laughing, however, and Boduur refused to laugh. When – in spite of herself – she laughed, she would ask God's refuge from Evil Satan and hide her mouth beneath her palm, saying 'May You restore all good, O Lord.'

Despite the resemblance between them, Boduur and Fawqiyya were like two antithetical poles, gravitating towards one another, repelling each other, competing for leadership of the cell. They differed in their outlooks on life and their concepts of the movement of history. Boduur believed that God was the mover of everything, and Fawqiyya considered that economic organisation was god.

'Disbeliever!' Boduur would scream out. 'Atheist! You don't even make one bow in prayer to God.'[1]

And the conflict between them would break out; the repulsion would be mutual. Soon enough, though, the opposite poles would be attracted to each other.

They were similar in features, traits, the desire for authority and the flight from taking on responsibilities. Both exerted themselves to achieve control over the cell, and both tried to escape responsibility and work.

They made a distinction between authority and responsibility. It was Boduur's view that God holds authority over everything and has supreme hegemony over all that life contains, whether good or evil. At the same time, God is only responsible for the good, in Boduur's view, while the Devil is to blame for all the evil and inequity in the world.

Fawqiyya thought that a leader holds no responsibility for small tasks such as washing the dishes after meals. There must be servants in attendance so the leader can eat, rest after eating, and then give a speech to the masses. She sanctified leadership like a god. And a god never errs; it bears responsibility for victory alone. Defeat,

---

[1] *rakaa* ('bow') is actually a sequence of motions and postures – bending, standing straight, prostrating oneself twice – accompanied by prescribed verses from the Qur'an. Each ritual prayer (carried out five times every day) consists of a certain number of *rakaas*.

however, stems from a lack of consciousness among the masses!

Each of us used to wash her own plate after eating and air her own bed after sleeping – except Fawqiyya and Boduur, who always awaited Dhuba's arrival so that she could do their work for them. If Dhuba did not show up, the plate remained dirty, tossed into the basin until someone else came along and washed it, and the bed stayed mussed, covered in flies and dirt until one of the other prisoners aired it.

We had no hot water. We were obliged to bathe in a cold shower. But not Boduur and Fawqiyya: they absolutely had to have hot water. And Dhuba must carry the bucket on her head, bringing hot water from the tap beneath the chimney. If there was no hot water for a week or more, Fawqiyya and Boduur would go without bathing. Their clothes remained unwashed, too, until Dhuba came.

No sooner did Dhuba appear than Boduur called out to her: 'Where is the hot water? For a week now, I've been requesting hot water so I can have a bath. Am I going to go for a fortnight in this horrid weather without bathing?' Fawqiyya would hand Dhuba a pile of dirty laundry, saying in the tone of one accustomed to ordering servants about, 'Wash my clothes, quickly now, and spread them in the sun, out in the enclosure, so they'll dry out before the *shawisha* locks us in.'

'She's a spy!' shrieked Boduur one day.

'How do you know she's a spy?' asked one of the other *munaqqabas*. 'Do you have any evidence?'

'God is my evidence,' replied Boduur, moving the rosary in her hand.

'Was it God who told you she's a spy?'

'Yes.'

The other responded, 'But God told me she's not a spy.'

'God speaks only to those with pure hearts!' Boduur said angrily.

'My heart is purer than yours!' the *munaqqaba* shouted.

'Shut up, you Farmawiyya!' yelled Boduur.

'I'm a Farmawiyya?! You Khomeiniyya! You Alawite!'

They began exchanging strange accusations which we had never heard before, and names which had never reached our ears. I heard one say to the other 'You Samawiyya!' and I thought she was accusing the other of putting poison – in Arabic, *samm* – in the food. It became clear to me later, though, that 'Samawi' is the name of a leader of one of the Islamic groups, as is 'Farmawi'.

'The Internal Security police always put a spy in every cell to relay the news to them.'

'Why should Itidaal be the spy, rather than one of the others?' I asked.

Another cellmate spoke up. 'She's a poor, luckless, miserable young girl who has no one.'

'That's the sort they always use,' replied Fawqiyya. 'They choose a poor one so they can entice her with money. Poverty weakens one's resistance when faced with the temptation of money.'

'Not always,' I said. 'The opposite is true, too. Wealth can make a person even more eager to acquire money. We can't accuse her without any evidence.'

Another cellmate spoke up. 'This is an injustice like the wrong done to us. Here we are in prison and they've decided we're guilty of conspiracy against the nation and of causing the sectarian rift, when they have no proof. Are we going to deal with her in a way that we reject and curse daily? How can her poverty be the single justification for your suspicion of her? You're the one who defends the poor!'

'Itidaal is a pious girl who wears a *niqaab*,' said a *munaqqaba*. 'She's not a spy.'

'Not everyone who has put on a *niqaab* is a true believer!' shouted Boduur. The quarrel began again . . . and the accusations . . . and the hysterical convulsions . . . and there was no place to flee, whether by night or by day.

I had imagined prison to be solitude and total silence, the isolated cell in which one lives alone, talking to oneself, rapping at the wall to hear the responding knock of one's neighbour. Here, though, I enjoyed neither solitude nor silence, except in the space after midnight and before the dawn call to prayer. I could not pull a door shut between me and the others, even when I was in the toilet.

If Boduur ceased quarrelling with her colleagues, she would begin reciting the Qur'an out loud. And if Boduur went to sleep, Fawqiyya would wake up and begin to discuss and orate. If

Fawqiyya went to sleep, Boduur would wake up to announce prayertime and the onset of night.

One night, the quarrel between Boduur and one of her comrades continued until dawn, ending only when Boduur fainted after she'd been hit by violent nervous convulsions. She tore at her hair and face with her fingernails, screaming until she lost consciousness.

As soon as the *shawisha* had opened the cell door in the morning, I called out to her. 'I want to be transferred to a solitary cell. I don't want to stay in this cell any longer.'

But the prison administration rejected my request. I came to understand that in prison, torture occurs not through solitude and silence but in a far more forceful way through uproar and noise. The solitary cell continued to float before me like a dream unlikely to be realised.

Since childhood, I've had a passion for solitude. I've not had a room in which I could shut myself off, for the number of individuals in every stage of my life has been greater than the number of rooms in the house. But I have always wrested for myself a place in which I could be alone to write. My ability to write has been linked to the possibility of complete seclusion, of being alone with myself, for I am incapable of writing when I am unable to give myself completely to solitude.

After midnight, when the atmosphere grows calm and I hear only the sound of sleep's regular breathing, I rise from my bed and tiptoe to the corner of the toilet, turn the empty jerry can upside down and sit on its bottom. I rest the aluminium plate on my knees, place against it the long, tape-like toilet paper, and begin to write.

In prison, a person's essence comes to light. One stands naked before oneself, and before others. Masks drop and slogans fall. In prison, one's true metal is revealed, particularly in times of crisis.

The warden gave one of our cellmates a body search and came upon a small piece of paper. It was nothing more than a short letter that she had written to her family, asking after their health and reassuring them of hers. However, the prison administration raged. There must be a pen and paper in the political cell! The search team attacked us – opening suitcases, overturning mattresses, stripping off *higaabs*, *niqaabs*, and cloaks.

One of the *munaqqabas* let out a scream – 'Infidels!' – when they uncovered her hair in front of the male prison administrators. They took her away to the disciplinary cell. From afar, we heard her screaming and we knew they had beaten her. We threatened collectively to go on a hunger strike until she was returned to us, and as a sort of protest against her beating. Collectively, that is, except Boduur and Fawqiyya.

'Going on strike is a type of protest and I do not participate in any protest against the authorities,' said Boduur. 'I do not address the tyrant – I only speak to God. I complain to no one. Complaining to anyone but God is a debasement!'

'They will face the strike by oppressing us still more,' was Fawqiyya's comment. 'Maybe they will put us all in correction cells and beat us.'

However, the group rejected Boduur's logic and that of Fawqiyya alike. The prison regulations do not permit beating or body searches. We must proclaim our rejection of this treatment and our protest. If we are silent this time, our silence will encourage them to repeat the insulting treatment and the beating. Let us use any weapon which we have between our hands. Even if it is merely depriving ourselves of food.

We failed to persuade Boduur. 'There is no point in making any protest,' she said in a tone of finality. 'They are tyrants. God will crush them if it is His wish.'

But Fawqiyya was more frank. The cellmates surrounded her with questions and asked how she could not submit to majority rule, when it was she who had touted the slogan of collective work and sacrifice for the sake of others. She said in a feeble voice, which was unlike any tone we'd heard from her previously, 'I am ill and I can't endure the strike.' She lay down on her bed moaning and complaining of a pain in her chest.

The door of the cell opened suddenly and we saw the *shawisha* entering, followed by our cellmate. We all jumped up to hug her, happy to see her return to us.

Fawqiyya jumped out of bed and embraced her, too, and in the act of leaping she forgot that she was ill.

Before dawn, I awoke to Boduur's voice.

'Get up! Arise for prayer! Prayer is better than sleep!'

'I'm not asleep,' she said in a listless voice. 'I'm sick. They beat me here . . . on my head . . . Men and women carrying thick, heavy sticks . . . I didn't see their faces . . . I heard their voices, though . . . They pulled off my *niqaab* and *higaab* . . . my hair came down in front of them . . . I hid it with my hands, my arms. Let them beat me to death but I will not allow men to see my hair! They pulled me by the hair down on to the ground, and put their hands all around my neck so I nearly choked. They stamped on my glasses . . . and I can't see at all without my glasses . . . I have an awful headache . . . my whole body is aching . . . my head . . . my neck . . . my spine . . .'

Boduur's voice came back. 'Get up and wash so you can perform the prayer, and don't say that you're ill! Prayer cures you of sickness. It is God who heals. Don't write any complaint to anyone. God is present. If you are innocent, God will make you victorious. Do not say that you didn't do anything wrong: you must have done something sinful in your life and then forgotten about it. God could not possibly expose you to pain or torture or prison or beating without a sin on your part. A human being is always sinful and you must ask God's forgiveness. Repentance is an obligation, whether you've committed a sin or not. Since God has requested us to ask His forgiveness, we must have committed sins. Human beings are sinful by nature – otherwise, there would be no such thing as repentance or forgiveness. Say "I beg God's forgiveness" three times, and get up to pray! You absolutely must stay up all night to pray – the five obligatory prayers are not enough. If you find the water cut off, intention is enough. The religion makes things easy, not difficult, and washing with water is not obligatory. Water is not important. It is important, though, that you keep God in your mind and speech, day and night. Staying up at night to pray is better and more enduring than sleep. You went to the correction cell because you were not staying up at night to pray and because you haven't memorised the Qur'an. I've told you more than once that you must learn two chapters of the Qur'an by heart every week. This is a sacred duty. Whoever does not fulfil it must have her feet whipped fifty times. Who knows, maybe it was God's will that you were beaten by the hands of others so you would atone for your sins. It's not enough that you cover your face with a *niqaab*. You must cleanse your heart of Satan's whisperings. Woman is nearer to Satan than man – through Eve, Satan was able to reach Adam. Woman was created from a crooked rib and she becomes straightened only through blows which hurt. Her duty is to listen and obey without making any objections – even a blink or a scowl. A scowl calls for thirty lashes on the feet.

I saw the girl rise from her bed. I saw her walk, her back stooped, in the direction of the toilet, groping for a way with her hands, for she had lost her glasses. She put on her cloak and *niqaab* . . . and stood behind Boduur, praying and asking God's forgiveness for her sins.

Shawisha Nabawiyya astonished me sometimes by taking courageous stands in which she stood firmly on the side of right and showed no fear of the prison administration's power. Unlike the other *shawishas*, she did not accept any bribery. Nor did she allow a prisoner to be beaten, even if the senior official in charge ordered her to do so.

'Once I obeyed the order and beat a prisoner in the correction cell,' she said. 'Then I went home, and I felt pain around my heart. I stayed home for a week, sick, and since then I have not beaten any prisoner. Even if they threatened to dismiss me, I would never beat a prisoner. I quarrel with my son when he beats a cat or dog – so what about a human being?'

Boduur was sitting beside her, listening to her words. 'You have a good heart, *Shawisha* Nabawiyya, and God will reward you well. God has requested us to show gentleness towards animals and human beings and all of God's creatures.'

'Except for one,' I remarked. 'Woman.'

'Why woman?' asked the *shawisha*.

'Because she was created from a crooked rib,' I replied, 'and only straightens up through beating.' I laughed, and so did the *shawisha* and the others in the cell – all except Boduur. Without delay, the scowl appeared on her forehead in the form of a deep, vertical line. 'Woman lacks intelligence and religion,' she said.

'And you? Aren't you a woman?' asked the *shawisha*.

'No!' she shouted.

Part III
Piercing the Blockade

As I stood behind the steel door, I could see dawn breaking through the covering of night. Pressing my nose between the thick black bars, I sniffed a breeze of fresh air. I remembered the sight of the imprisoned lion in the Cairo Zoo . . . thrusting his large head between the steel columns, then pacing round and round inside the bars without cease. I recalled, too, the sight of the wolf inside his steel cage and the tiger and all the other animals.

I look at my fingers, clutching the steel bars. My fingernails have grown and lengthened – they look like claws now. I haven't cut them since I came to prison. Scissors are among the prohibited items, since they are considered sharp implements. I contemplate my fingers in astonishment. I've never had such fingernails, ever! Are they my own fingernails or the claws of an animal?

My hair has grown, too; it touches my neck and shoulders by now. Thick, tousled hair like a lion's mane. I probe my face; under my hand, I feel my nose extending between the steel bars, as if it has lengthened to become like an elephant's trunk! I have forgotten the shape of my face; I haven't seen it in a mirror since I entered prison. Mirrors are among the prohibited items, since they are considered sharp implements.

I touch my arms and legs. The skin is dark brown, and across it run lines of red and blue, like fingernail marks. Do I scratch at night, while I'm asleep? Has scabies infection been transmitted to me?

I stretch my nose outside the bars . . . through it I escape far from the odour of burnt gas, the rotting garbage in the corners, and the dampness of the cement floor and tiles. I remain standing behind the bars; I sense the fatigue in my body due to standing for so long. I bend my body to sit upon the hard ground. I rest my body against the bars. I remain seated, still like the wall. Time, too is like the wall.

I feel tired due to such a long period of sitting. I unroll my body and get to my feet. I stroll around the cell. All of my cellmates are asleep. Dawn prayer has not yet been announced. Boduur is still sleeping, her features given over to sadness. All the bodies have gone lax, faces pale and faded in a complete submission to a long, sad, sleep.

My heart is heavy . . . how long will time stretch on for us in this grave? Time does not budge, like this mangy ceiling over my head from which dangles an electric light, flaming day and night like a bulging red eye, with a black rope wound round its neck on to which cling flies – sleeping or dead.

How long have I been in this steel cage? When was the first night? Since Sunday, 6 September, and what is today? I don't know the day of the week, or the date, or the hour. In prison one loses one's sense of the date, and of time itself.

I've been here for a long time . . . for a century . . . a thousand years . . . since I was born and since I became aware of something called time . . . Ever since they broke down the door by force and carried me off in the van on this unknown voyage through the darkness.

Since that day I've been here and no one has told me why. No one has directed any charges at me, and the only answer I have had to any of my questions is: 'We are awaiting instructions from above. We are awaiting new orders.'

What are the old orders, then? The Precautionary Detention Order! And what does 'the Precautionary Detention Order' signify? It means imprisonment inside a cell, behind bars, without an investigation, without letters from home or visits, without newspapers or radio or going out into the prison courtyard. Complete, absolute imprisonment without human or legal rights. Absolute imprisonment which will end no one knows when, except one man, the one who issued the Precautionary Detention Order. And he is the sole person able to cancel or alter it.

For the first time, the meaning of 'autocracy' is embodied before me. For the first time, dictatorship takes tangible form before my eyes. Previously, I had rejected it as an idea, a style, and a system of organisation. But now I came to reject it with my entire being, with all the longing I feel for life and freedom, with my soul and body alike. Yet how does such a rejection begin to assume the form of positive action? How do I break through the blockade thrown up around my mind and body? I cannot pull my body out between the steel bars . . . but I can extract my mind.

The idea of breaking through the blockade began to take me captive. I whispered to Fathiyya-the-Murderess: 'Fathiyya, I want to send a letter to my family . . . is that possible?'

'Everything is possible,' she whispered.

'Inside prison?' I said out loud, in astonishment.

She laughed. 'Inside prison is just like outside prison. Everything is possible . . . what's important is the determination to do it.'

'I am determined!' I said.

'Your will is like mine,' she said, laughing again. 'When I decide to do something . . . Oh God . . .'

I spent an entire night writing a letter to my family – to my husband, son, and daughter. It was a long letter, into which I emptied all that was in my head.

The days and nights went by, and still I received no reply. My eyes would meet Fathiyya's gaze, and I would say nothing. The *shawisha*'s eyes were always observant, and her ears were sharp. In her eyes was a look of suspicion and doubt . . . and Fathiyya avoided looking my way. Why was she afraid to look me in the eye? Had I put my confidence in the wrong place? Had Fathiyya given my letter to the *shawisha*, or to the administrators of the prison?

It is not my nature to harbour suspicions. As far as I am concerned, a person is innocent until proven guilty. Whenever I looked into Fathiyya's eyes, I felt that she was sincere; she was a woman of courage and decency. Were my perceptions deceptive? I've always trusted my subconscious perceptions, and I don't distinguish between intellect and feelings. Sound feelings mean a sound mind. Sometimes the intellect errs, knowing only numbers and the circumscribed logical thinking which we inherit and to which we become accustomed. But sound feelings represent the more profound mind – that which comprises human sentiment, emotional feelings, perception and discernment and the accumulation of knowledge and experience.

Day after day, though, the doubt was growing in my mind. Perhaps I had sketched features from my imagination to place over the real Fathiyya. Maybe, after all, she was a spy!

The blood rushed to my face. I felt sudden terror. I lost confidence in my ability to judge people and things.

I sensed myself falling, disintegrating, my heart pounding, my throat dry. My fingers were trembling. Fawqiyya smiled triumphantly and whispered in my ear: 'I told you she was a spy. Everyone who comes into our cell here is a spy. Don't trust anyone.'

The walls and steel bars were folding in on me from all sides. Doubt and burnt gas choked me. I did not see human faces, but only expanses of blackness, holes from which gazed eyes as red as those of devils. The face of Fathiyya came to resemble Satan's countenance. Murderess, daughter of a murderess, as the *shawisha* would say. For me, she'd injected poison into her honeyed words.

I tossed and turned upon the wooden board, unable to close an eyelid. I became aware that torture in prison does not take place by means of the bars, or the walls, or the stinging insects, or hunger or thirst or insults or beating.

Prison is doubt. And doubt is the most certain of tortures. It is doubt that kills the intellect and body – not doubt in others, but doubt in oneself . . . The baffling, crushing question for the mind: was I right or wrong? Had Fawqiyya been correct in her doubts? Had my judgement been in error?

I opened my eyes in the morning to the sound of the key turning three times in the door. I did not get out of bed; I did not carry out my daily exercises; I did not take a shower or drink tea. I stayed in bed, bitterness in my throat and a painful lump in my heart.

'How odd!' my astonished cellmates remarked. 'Are you ill?'

'If the doctor has got sick,' someone said, 'this is the end.'

'We've all been sick except you,' another called out, 'so your turn has come now!'

Not one of them really believed that I was ill. But no sooner did they glance at my face than silence fell. I did not know what my face looked like.

'Shall we call the doctor?' I heard a sympathetic voice ask. 'Can I make a cup of tea?' inquired another voice, even gentler.

Even Boduur and Fawqiyya – I saw them at my side. For the first time, I saw a kind smile on Boduur's face, a smile like that of a mother to her child. I heard her say, 'I'll give you a blanket of mine, you must have caught a cold.'

And the deep furrow in Fawqiyya's forehead all but disappeared as she said gently, 'I told you to keep up your health more carefully! It's that cold shower every day that has made you ill.'

And *Shawisha* Nabawiyya placed her thin hand on my head. 'Looks like we've put the evil eye on you, by God. I'll say the Verse of Yasin for you.'

And I saw Fathiyya's face. I shut my eyes.

I don't want to see her.

But she drew near and whispered in my ear. 'I have a letter for you.'

I leapt out of bed.

She preceded me, her gait fast and her stride long, to the toilet. She raised her white *gallabiyya* and extended her hand beneath to undo a sash around her abdomen. My heart jumped from beneath my ribs when I saw the folded piece of paper between her fingers. I threw my arms around her, almost choking her. 'Read it quickly,' she whispered, 'then throw it into the toilet.'

I stood in the cramped lavatory, which was reeking with the stench of rot. I stood on the footrests on either side of the hole which overflowed with sewer water and cockroaches, my back to the black, fissured wall and before me the half of broken door. I stood there, neither smelling the odour nor seeing the black wall, unaware of where I was. I stood, opening the folded paper, my fingers shaking, my heart pounding with thousands of sensations. My eyes, unfocused and wandering, could not see the letters. I was not wearing reading glasses, and the letters jumped before my eyes as if there were water between me and them.

I rubbed my eyes on my *gallabiyya* sleeve. Tears, I realised. The letters began to appear clearly. I recognised my husband's handwriting, and that of my daughter, and then my son's hand. My breaths were coming fast, as if I were gulping for air. Blood constricted my chest, and my heartbeat was like the rapping of drums. I brought the paper near and sniffed it . . . the odour of my son, my daughter, my husband . . . the scent of my house, of my books and papers and bed . . . the aroma of my whole life, which the night of my entrance to prison had stripped from my memory.

'My beloved wife . . . dearest mum . . . mama, my love . . .'

I stopped a bit to catch my breath and wipe away my tears, then I read the letter all at once. I memorised it, phrase by phrase, so that I would be able to repeat it to myself, so that every letter and every word would be etched on my memory before I burnt it.

I lit a match and brought it to the edge of the paper. My eyes followed the lines as they burned, word by word, letter by letter, until the end. The remains floated, like the flecks of black, over the stinking hole in the ground.

That night I closed my eyes and imagined the letter before me. I began to hear the warm voice speaking. 'The three of us returned to the house that night and discovered the door broken, and found that you weren't there. We were terrified. What had happened to you? We went out into the street to search for you and met one of the neighbours. He told us that a number of armed policemen had broken down the door and taken you away in their van. No one knew where. We searched for you in the district police stations, and in the Internal Security Police Bureau. No one knew anything. One of the guards said to us, "Go and look in Tura Prison." We went but we didn't find you there. We read in the newspapers that the authority responsible for the matter was the Bureau of the Socialist Prosecutor, in the Ministry of Justice building at Lazoghli Square. We went there the next day, and saw a long queue of mothers and fathers and spouses and other family members . . . a long queue, standing before one of the entrances. We stood with them all day long. Then we went up a flight of stairs at the back of the large building – like a servants' staircase. We entered by a door leading into a long corridor, in which an office boy, or errand boy, was sitting behind a small desk, a number of application forms in front of him. He raised his head and asked us "What do you want?" We told him we wanted to know where you were. He riffled through the forms then pulled one from among them. "Fill out this request form and leave it here on the desk. Come back in a couple of days to take the number of the request." One of the fathers searching for their sons barked, "These requests are no use! I'll go and look myself." At the end of the day, we left the building and began the search. For eight whole days we continued to look for you. Then we heard that you were in the Barrages Women's Prison. We came to the prison and left a suitcase for you with the people in charge, containing clothes and sports shoes. Exercise in prison is essential. We still can't believe what has happened. It was a great shock to us. Since your absence we've been flooded with telegrams and telephone calls from all corners of the globe. There's been a major international campaign in your support and demonstrations held by women in front of Egyptian embassies, calling for your release. The Writers' and Journalists' Unions, the literati, and everyone who has read your books and novels, have also been active. There is a campaign going on in support of you and all of those who have been imprisoned. And people here, too, have been asking after you every day – and neighbours, friends, and relatives. Your position is very strong, for you are an independent writer, a well-known novelist, and a fighter for the rights of women and the freedom of humankind.

'The Socialist Prosecutor has begun the investigations. We've engaged the services of an excellent lawyer for you. To this day, the lawyer has not learned the nature of the charges against you, and he does not know the day or the hour in which you'll appear for investigation before the Socialist Prosecutor. But he goes every day to the Bureau of the Socialist Prosecutor so that he'll be waiting for you whenever you arrive. Question the investigator about your connection with the sectarian rift, since that is the official reason published in the newspapers to justify the detentions. We meet with the lawyer daily, and we'll send you summaries of his opinions. The lawyer says not to worry, and that he will be with you during the investigation. He anticipates that the investigation is not likely to deal with your books but rather with the articles which you have written for the opposition newspapers. We will search for these articles among your papers and send copies of them to you so you can review them before the investigation. We would have liked the trial to be public so people could hear your views, but the trials are not being announced publicly. Take care of your health. We are all well and we think about you all the time. We love you and we are waiting for you to come back to us!'

When I'd finished reading my letter I put on my sports shoes and began my exercises. The strenuous athletic movements evolved into motions as near as could be to the movements of dance. The *shawisha* looked me in the eye and said in an astonished voice, 'Good heavens! An hour ago, you were ill. I've sent for the doctor.'

'Doctor?' I queried in amazement. 'What doctor can cure me when I'm a doctor myself?'

'The prison doctor!' she replied.

'Am I in prison?'

'By God's holy greatness! Where are you, then?'

'I'm in the heavens, *shawisha*.' I could hear the birds singing in the air.

If the unrestrained voices which defend freedom of opinion and speech had been raised all over the world to demand my release and that of everyone who had been put in prison without trial, accusation, or a crime, why hadn't a single voice from within Egypt been raised? Have mouths been muzzled to this extent? Has fright settled so permanently in people's minds and souls?

From the prison, I sent a letter to the Egyptian Syndicate of Physicians – in my capacity as a member – and I also sent a letter to the Writers' Union, requesting that they delegate someone to take a stand opposing the situation we were living through in prison and to demand our release or at least our presentation to a fair and public trial.

No one sent me any reply, however . . . rather, I got a complete silence . . . this was utter disregard of our presence in prison.

Not even a single writer from among my colleagues and friends published one word in defence of freedom of opinion and speech. They shrank inside their homes, taking refuge in silence and inaction, or travelling abroad, or sharing with others in playing on the strings which give pleasure to the holders of power.

I saw her black eyes looking at me. I followed her quickly to the toilet enclosure. She lifted her white *gallabiyya* and handed me a small white envelope. She said, gasping for breath, 'Don't forget – burn everything after you read it.'

I opened the envelope, finding some printed papers and a small piece of paper on which the following words were written:

'We're searching for the articles you've published in the opposition newspapers, the ones that might be taken up in the investigation. We're sending these articles to you. One is entitled "It is the people who form the parties"; this was published in *Al Shaab* (The People) Newspaper, 9 November 1981. The second was published under the title "On the Problem of Press Freedom", appearing also in *Al Shaab*, on 27 January 1981; the third is called "The Rulers Form Governments and the People Wear Dunce's Caps"[1] published in *Al Ahali* (The Populace) Newspaper on 12 April 1978. The lawyer thinks the investigation might deal with these articles or possibly any article you've published since 1970. We'll look for the others. We're also sending you a copy of the text of the resignation which you presented to the Minister of Health on 16 January 1981, since the investigator might question you about it. The lawyer asks that you study these papers carefully. We are all well; we lack only your presence among us. We love you!'

[1]The verb used here to mean 'to form governments', *yu'allifuna*, can also take the meaning 'to invent (stories, etc.)'.

Part IV
Out to the Investigation

I heard my name echo through the air . . . and a voice saying, 'You've been requested to appear at this time before the Socialist Prosecutor for investigation.'

It was as if I'd just learnt that I was released! Friends and the other cellmates jumped up to surround me, with congratulations, hugs, and exclamations. 'The investigation has started, and now we'll all be leaving, released!' 'The truth has begun to come out!' 'God is great!' 'Go and God be with you.' I accepted the congratulations and kisses, my heart beating wildly as I paced the cell, my cellmates bunched around me. Surprise, joy, a glimmer of hope . . .

'Put on your street clothes, now, hurry, the police officers are waiting for you in the *ma'mur*'s office,' said the warden.

'Why didn't they inform me far enough in advance so I could prepare myself?'

'If you're late,' replied the warden, 'They'll go away and the investigation session will be lost to you.'

All of the cellmates ran off to bring me things. One brought me my comb, another came with my dress. Someone began combing my hair while another helped me into the white dress in which I'd left home on the night of my arrest. Still another handed me half of a pitta loaf encasing a bit of cheese. 'Don't go the investigation on an empty stomach.' Her voice reminded me of my mother's, when she used to hand me a sandwich and tell me in the same way, 'Don't go to the examination on an empty stomach.'

My heartbeat is rapid, resembling the way my heart used to beat when I was a young student in secondary school on my way to an examination. Last night, I dreamt that I was sitting among the pupils, the examination questions before me. I did not know the answer to a single question. It is a dream which has repeated itself at every stage of my life, even in prison.

One of the cellmates handed me a cup of tea. My throat was parched . . . I began to sip the tea.

'The officers are waiting!' shouted the warden. 'I'll go after I've drunk my tea,' I said calmly. 'They should have sent me a notice yesterday. What sort of investigation is this, which is run secretly and by surprise too?'

I drained the cup of tea and went with the warden to the *ma'mur*'s office. I saw a crowd of armed men led by an officer. I recalled the day on which they had arrested me . . . Baffled, I remarked, 'Am I all that dangerous?'

I saw the main prison door flung open as wide as could be. In front of it were police vans which resembled the vehicles that had stopped before my house on the sixth of September. It was the same awesome procession, preceded by a man on a motorcycle clearing the road . . . and a police siren . . . and a troop of armed soldiers . . . who jumped into the vehicles that took up the rear.

The officer demanded that I sit between him and the driver. I refused. The scene repeats itself, and so do the words. 'These are the orders.'

'I will only sit next to the window.'

A look of determination came over him, and a look of greater determination appeared on my face. My persistence triumphed over his, and I sat by the window. A small, simple victory, but an important one, too. I am acting according to my own will despite everything!

The van left the narrow vault for a long one at the end of which was a thick pole blocking the way. The car stopped at the pole and from the side of the road appeared a thin man whose eyes gleamed and flashed like those of a highwayman. He took note of the motorcycle and vehicles and quickened his step, running with bent back to pull the pole upward. The police procession went through and the pole fell. The road was closed behind us.

I raised my head towards the road. The brilliant sun filled the street and the entire universe. Its light was strong and dazzling, painful to the eyes. From afar, the Barrages sparkled and the surface of the Nile shone under the sun. The odour of the Nile filled my nose as I took a whiff of a clear, fresh breeze carrying the scent of the vegetation.

I took a deep breath. Had I been dead and just awakened? Had I been buried and then emerged on to the earth's surface? The sight of people in the street was odd to me, and their movements were bewildering. My eyes widened as if I were seeing them for the first time in my life: a woman standing before a greengrocer, leaning over a basket of red tomatoes. The redness of tomatoes is startlingly beautiful! The hue of vegetables in the baskets was an amazing green. People were entering and leaving the shops in an awesomely peculiar fashion. The cars running over the asphalt . . . a woman driving a car, pressing forcefully on the horn . . . the voice of the horn resounding in my ears wierdly . . . all of the horns chanting sweet melodies . . . a man sitting in a café reading the newspaper, out in the open, without hiding it . . . the sound of a radio blaring from the café, audible to all passing ears . . . strange things I was hearing and seeing as if for the first time. How long has it been since I'd seen a street? I counted the days on my fingers . . . 22 days, which seemed to me more like 22 years or a century.

People on both sides of the street were gazing attentively at the police procession. Eyes showing amazement – whether the result of fear or of suppressed anger. Thin, pale faces. Bowed backs . . . lame legs walking slowly . . . There was something akin to despair in the movement of arms, and the eyes were marked by a lifeless sadness.

A face split with a sudden smile, and two hands went up waving a handkerchief. I waved. The officer barked in alarm, 'Please, do not speak to people!'

'I'm not speaking to people.'

The procession continued along the lengthy way, the Nile to my right and the fields on my left. It is a road carved in my memory. The driver's face is a pale brown, like those of my relatives, the peasants in Kafr Tahla. Black and white spots mark the hands and face. The hands are brown and cracked, clutching the steering column as if it is a hoe.

The officer takes off his police cap and places it on his knees. He looks straight ahead at the road. His head falls over his chest, and his lids drop over his eyes. The regular sound of snoring grows louder.

The van reached Liberation Square, in the middle of downtown Cairo. It turned off towards Lazoghli Square. The driver pressed hard on the brakes and the officer opened his eyes suddenly as if in terror, looked around and saw the immense structure which bears the inscription 'Ministry of Justice'. He wiped his mouth, put his cap on, and tautened the muscles of his face and body. He straightened the collar of his jacket and made sure the buttons were done up. We got out of the van, and so did the armed men.

Only the officer and one policeman entered the building with me. The others remained with the vans. I walked between the officer and the policeman, my head raised, standing taller than either of them. A man on my right and one to my left, just like aides-de-camp. I saw a queue of Ministry employees standing in front of the door to the lift, waiting. Their eyes widened as they stared in our direction. I smiled at them confidently. Their eyes shifted in fright and they swung their heads in the other direction, lowering them submissively, dejectedly – except for one head, whose eyes were firmly fixed on mine. He smiled encouragingly and gazed at the officer with an angry and threatening mien.

The officer headed towards another lift, designated specially for the Minister and important visitors. The lift attendant raised his hand in greeting and cleared the way for the officer. I followed the officer into the lift, and behind me entered the police guard. The officer pressed 7 and the lift ascended . . . stopped . . . the officer went out, I stepped out after him, and the guard came after me. The officer walked down a long corridor lined with numerous offices and closed doors in front of which were sitting a number of office attendants and errand boys. The officer stopped and spoke with one of them, then retraced his steps towards the lift, saying 'Not this floor.'

The lift wasn't there. The officer glanced apprehensively at his watch and said, breaking into a run, 'Let's take the stairs.' We ran behind him, myself and the guard.

On the ninth floor, they waved him down to the fifth floor . . .

We descended behind him at a run. He was gasping for breath, and so were we. On the fifth floor, one of the office boys said: 'Go up to the eighth floor.' The officer took off at a run for the stairs. I stopped and called out in anger, 'This is incredible! I'm not going to budge.'

'Never mind, doctor,' said the officer imploringly. 'No one told me exactly where the investigation would be, and it's a big building.'

'Doesn't anyone know where the Bureau of the Socialist Prosecutor is?' I asked, baffled.

'It isn't just one office. It's many offices, distributed across several floors.'

We went up to the eighth floor, which resembled the levels to which we had already been – the long corridor lined by closed doors, office help and errand boys sitting in front of every door, some sleeping, others eating. A young woman was running along the corridor followed by a child with a fly-laden face and a runny nose.

Just before we reached the end of the corridor, the officer stopped before an open door. I saw a large chamber full of officers and policemen. Just inside the door was a long wooden bench on which armed soldiers were sitting. All the eyes in that place were staring at me, and then the eyelids dropped in a resemblance of drowsiness or a stupor.

The officer exchanged a few words with the chief of officers then led me to another room at the end of the corridor.

I'm walking with slow steps, doubting that I am awake. Maybe I'm dreaming, or perhaps I'm watching a play or a chapter from Kafka's novel *The Trial*. The calendar on the wall indicates that today is the 28 September, 1981. The room is packed with men and youths, some in long beards and moustaches, wearing *gallabiyyas*, others cleanshaven and short-cropped, wearing suits. Some sitting, hands free, next to a guard, and others attached with iron chains to their guards.

Eyes stared when I came in. Some of those in beards and *gallabiyyas* bowed their heads, averting their eyes. Other eyes recognised my face. One man called out, 'Welcome, doctor . . . is this the first time you've come out for investigation?'

'Yes. And you?'

'This is my third time. And every time, the investigation lasts five hours. The Socialist Prosecutor asks me about words I said twenty years ago.'

Those in suits laughed. The bearded heads nodded; a faint smile intimating shared experience clothed their faces.

'I expect they'll ask me about my childhood, then,' I said.

'Everything is possible,' he said, laughing. 'Anything can happen these days.'

I saw an officer enter the room. He called me to go out into the corridor with him. My guard followed.

Pointing to a chair in the corridor, the officer said, 'You can wait here until your turn comes for investigation.'

I refused to sit down, and to the officer I said in a tone of anger, 'This is a corridor, not a waiting room!'

'There is no empty room.'

'Then I'll go back to the room I was in. I'll sit there.'

'That's for the men.'

'Why don't you designate a room specially for women? If it's absolutely necessary to separate the sexes.'

'There aren't enough rooms.'

'I will not sit in the corridor.'

'We don't have any other place.'

I rushed off angrily – the guard behind me – to the officers' room. I headed straight for their chief, who was sitting at an enormous desk.

'I will only sit in a room as the others are doing. I don't care whether I sit by myself or with others – men – but I will absolutely not sit in the corridor.'

They searched for a room but found none, and in the face of my determination they were forced to let me return to sit in the waiting room.

The men welcomed my return with the warmth of comradeship and participation in a shared ordeal. I felt that they were all my comrades – we were united by a single destiny. I sensed that even those youths in long beards and *gallabiyyas* who had averted their gaze were regarding me as a comrade who had been imprisoned with them.

A young girl of about thirteen came in wearing a country *gallabiyya* and plastic sandals on her cracked feet, carrying a tray of small cups of tea. After she had distributed the tea to those in the room, she turned to me. 'Shall I bring you a cup of tea?'

'From where?'

'From the buffet.'

'What buffet?'

'The Ministry buffet.'

The buffet of the Ministry of Health, where I had worked for several years, returned to my memory. The buffet had been inside the lavatory; the flies would move from the basin to the cups. One of the office attendants or errand boys was in charge of making the tea and coffee. He never washed the cups and glasses and he filled the pitcher from the lavatory tap.

'No thanks,' I said.

'Impossible!' one of the comrades called out. 'You must have something to drink before the investigation. Bring her a cup of tea!'

'I have no money,' I said.

'None of us has any money. Everything is put on account.'

'The lawyers pay me,' said the girl. 'Don't you have a lawyer?'

'Yes, I have a lawyer, but I don't know whether or not he has arrived.'

'Give me his name,' she said. 'I'll ask about him. All the lawyers wait below, in the basement.'

I gave her the name and she left hurriedly. I heard the fellow prisoner who was sitting beside me speak. 'If your lawyer hasn't come, don't worry. It's merely a pro forma investigation, just to establish that there is a law. But the law is on holiday, doctor!'

'Hasten to prayer!' muttered a youth with a full black beard and small blackish eyes. The youths got to their feet, even those whose wrists were bound to the wrists of their guards. The guards undid the chains with small keys and the whole group rose to pray. They removed their sandals and stood in a single row behind the prayer leader, their shoulders pressed together and their feet touching. The prayer leader raised his hands to touch his ears and called out, '*Allahu akbar*, God is greatest.'

They raised their hands to touch their ears repeating the call in unison. 'God is greatest . . .'

From the corridor rang out a voice calling a name. One of the fellow prisoners rose, his guard standing up behind him, as the others called out to him:

'The Prosecutor, today, will ask you about the Second World War!'

'Don't worry,' he replied, laughing. 'I have four lawyers with me!'

The laughs rang out . . . and abruptly, they stopped laughing. They were suddenly overwhelmed by a feeling of sadness, as if they had just remembered that they were prisoners and that after the investigation they would return to prison. Or, perhaps they realised that laughter is not appropriate when prayer is in progress. The youths from the Islamic groups were still performing the series of ritual prayer movements – kneeling, prostrating and rising, then kneeling again – all the while murmuring verses from the Qur'an.

A silence that hinted sadness and dread descended on the group. Next to me, I heard a sound which could have been snoring. I saw two youths, seated, who had not risen to perform the ritual prayer. They looked so much alike that they could have been twins – their faces were long, pale, and blotched, and their eyes wandered blankly, staring into empty space. They were chained together at the wrist. I realised then that one was a prisoner and the other was his guard, but the resemblance between them was peculiar. They had the same body movements, too – the head swaying a bit, then dropping over the chest, the exhausted and lacklustre eyes closing, then that commotion, like an unexpected alertness, eyelids springing open at the same instant, together, eyes widening momentarily in consternation or alarm. Then the lids would fall over the eyes once again, and the regular sound of snoring would return.

In the corner of the room, next to the window, I saw a man sitting in silence, reading the Bible. He was wearing a black cloak which resembled priestly garb. Around him, three men – heads shaking – moved their lips.

The room appeared before my eyes like a theatre stage on which a scene from the theatre of the absurd was unfolding.

Brows cemented to the floor. Palms raised high. Heads bowed low over chests. Murmurings of the Qur'an, murmurings of the Bible. Ample, flowing *gallabiyyas*. Elegant, stylish suits. Faces bare of beard or moustache, heads shaved. Faces covered with hair thick as forest regions. It appeared as though these people had nothing in common – except their presence now on the stage of this theatre.

A tall, broadly-built man wearing an elegant full suit entered the room. The face was that of an old man; it gazed down upon me from a faraway age, one rooted deeply in a time long since past. His stature and his manner of walking across the stage lent the impression that he was a man of dignity and authority, belied only by the presence of the guard who followed behind and gave the impression that this man was indeed one of the prisoners.

The men jumped to their feet.

'*Ahlan*, Pasha. Welcome.'

'*Tafaddul*, Pasha. Come in.'

'This seat, Pasha, is comfortable. Please, sit here.'

He sat down beside me. I'd seen his features many years before in the newspapers, on the front pages. At the time, I was a child, and while my father read his newspaper, I looked at the pictures – at the photographs of Nahhas Pasha and Fouad Serag al-Din Pasha. Nahhas's face was long and thin, and one of his eyes was smaller than the other. The smaller eye looked in my direction, and the larger one looked towards Serag al-Din. Serag al-Din's face was large, round, and fully-fleshed. His eyes were wide and stared straight ahead. I used to hear my father say 'Serag al-Din resembles the King. Nahhas, though, is from the people.'

My mother would reply, 'Nahhas was one of the poor folk, but he married Zaynab al-Wakil.'

Since childhood, then, I'd made a mental linkage between the name of the King and those of Serag al-Din, Zaynab al-Wakil, and Nahhas. When the King fell from power on 23 July 1952, they all fell with him – and so did the title of Pasha. Never in my life had I uttered the words 'Pasha' or 'Bey' or 'Effendi'. I had become accustomed to addressing people as 'Mister' or 'Doctor'.

'Have you greeted the Pasha?' I heard someone ask.

I shook his hand. 'Welcome, Mister Fouad Serag al-Din.'

The eyes widened in surprise. He turned towards me, shifting his whole body, and for the first time I saw his face. It was not the face which I used to see in the newspapers: his features did not resemble those of King Farouq. Despite old age, his eyes were lively, alert, and attentive.

'How are all of you faring in the women's prison?' he asked me.

'Do you sleep on the ground or on beds?'

'I sleep on a wooden board on top of a bedstead,' I said. 'And you? In the men's prison, do all of you sleep on the ground?'

'I slept on the ground for several days. I could only get to my feet with the help of three fellow inmates. Then the prison doctor came to me, and I requested that he get me a bed. The bed arrived. I demanded that the doctor examine it closely and tell me whether or not this was a bed. The doctor came in again, and after looking the bed over carefully, it became clear to him that it was only a wooden bench.'

Everyone laughed.

'We knew Fouad Pasha in prison,' one of the men said, 'and he was an example to us of endurance and the refusal to yield, as we saw him sitting proudly in the cell like a lion who feels no pain.'

'It's my good fortune that Egypt's best youths and men were with me in the cell,' said Serag al-Din. The conversation went on for a while. Serag al-Din was called in for investigation, and after him others were summoned. The buffet girl came in carrying cups of tea.

'So far, your lawyer hasn't shown up,' she told me.

'If he hasn't come, you can postpone the interrogation so that he can be here with you,' one of the fellow prisoners said. 'That's the better alternative for you – unless you know something about the law.'

'My knowledge of legal matters is sparse,' I said. 'I don't trust the fairness of the investigation, either.'

'We're all like you,' he said. 'This investigation is a political matter, not a legal one. The prosecutor will ask you what your political life has been since Sadat took over, and maybe before that, God only knows. Is this the first time you've gone to prison?'

'First time,' I said. 'And you? First time, too?'

'No, I entered prison in the days of the King and in the days of Nasser. This is the third time.'

'You're a vintage politician.'

'Ever since I was in secondary school, ever since the demonstrations of 1946,[1] I used to go out into the streets with the other

[1]Demonstrations of 1946: widespread demonstrations, riots, and looting in Cairo and Alexandria followed a demand by the Egyptian government of the time that the Anglo-Egyptian Treaty of 1936 be renegotiated and

students. We'd call out slogans against the King and the British. Perhaps you don't remember those demonstrations?'

'I remember them well. I was in secondary school.'

Old images came back to me. The boarding pupils' dormitory in Helwan School: the bell for sleep rang, and the electric light was extinguished. The matron spied on us to make sure we were sleeping. No sooner did the sound of her footfall in the corridor become distant then we jumped out of our beds and stayed up until morning, working by moonlight to weave these letters on to our tunics: 'Evacuation through blood'. In the morning, we gathered in the school courtyard, broke the lock on the school door and went out into the street shouting our slogans. At Helwan Station, we took over a whole train car which carried us to Bab al-Luq in the centre of Cairo, and from there we walked with the demonstrations of students as far as Abdin Square.[1] I went into Abdin Palace with a group of students, both male and female. It was the first time in my life I'd gone into anything like this palace. All I recall is that my shoes, which were covered in dust, sank into soft, deep carpets. There were very high fancily decorated carved walls, a large desk on which was a huge, open record book, and tall men wearing black suits, their muscles taut as if stretched by wires. They requested that we write out our names, and then we went back outside into the Square. The slogan-calling went on for a while before I returned to school with my schoolmates.

As soon as the school's matron saw me she pulled me from among the other girls with her strong, steely fingers and led me to the office of the superintendent. I heard the superintendent speak to my father over the telephone. She told him that the lightest penalty I could get would be dismissal from the school. At that, my mouth went dry and my heart began pounding. I loved school in spite of the matron. I loved both the sciences and Arabic literature, and I was intending to enter either the College of Arts or the College of Medicine. From the superintendent's manner of speaking, I realised that she respected my father. She addressed him by the title of

particularly that British troops be withdrawn from Egypt, which the British government refused to consider. Students and workers were at the forefront of the demonstrations.

[1] Abdin Square, in the centre of Cairo, is the site of the Government Palace – once the King's official seat of rule, now the centre of the state executive.

'Bey'. At that time, my father was an inspector in the Ministry of Education, and I used to see the superintendent and teachers reacting with apprehension whenever any inspector entered the school.

The superintendent did not dismiss me. I learned from my father that he had defended me. He had told the superintendent that the female students had the right to participate in the nationalist demonstrations just as much as the male students did. I learned also that the teachers, male and female, came to my defence because I was an excellent student.

In the College of Medicine, I used to go to the demonstrations with the male students. During one of the demonstrations, I found that I was the sole female student present, walking among the male students and carrying with them the huge placard on which we had inscribed 'Men and Women Students of Medicine'.

My father and mother used to encourage me to participate in the nationalist demonstrations against the King and the British. During the 1919 Revolution,[1] my father had been a student of Dar al-Ulum in Cairo, Egypt's major teacher training institute. In the company of some of his classmates, he participated in beating up a party of English soldiers. A bullet splinter wounded him in the leg, and he returned to his village, Kafr Tahla, carried on a donkey cart.

My mother had been a young pupil in elementary school in Cairo at that time. She went out into the street with some of the other girls from her school to call out slogans against the British. The police arrested her and kept her in the police station for a full day before she returned home.

I came to at the sound of my name reverberating through the air. I stood up. My guard came behind me, and before me walked an officer who led me to a tightly closed door. He opened it and I entered alone, the officer and guard remaining outside the door.

[1]The Paris Peace Conference, and particularly the Wilson doctrine of self-determination, raised the hopes of the Egyptian populace for independence and an end to the British occupation of Egypt. The nationalist leader Saad Zaghlul pushed this demand and was exiled by the British to Malta, along with two other leading nationalists. Throughout Egypt, demonstrations and riots turned into a full-scale revolt which was eventually quelled by the British through the use of force.

I found myself in an air-conditioned room. I filled my chest with the refreshing air. I saw a man sitting behind a large desk, and another sitting at a small table on which was a large record book like that of the local Muslim registry official in which he inscribes marriages, births and deaths.

The investigator called for me to sit down. I noticed that in front of him was an official government envelope sealed with red wax. Beside it lay a blue-covered file folder on which was written my name. He opened the dossier and the envelope and looked at the papers inside. I fixed my eyes on his face: it was a large, dark face, and he had widely spaced eyes which did not look directly into mine, as if he were anxious to avoid meeting my gaze. Why?

Why would he not look me straight in the eye?

'Your session was scheduled for yesterday,' I heard him say. 'Why did you fail to attend yesterday?'

My eyes widened in bewilderment. Was this investigator crazy? Or was it I that had gone mad and no longer understood what he was saying?

'What are you saying?' I asked in a voice which betrayed astonishment.

'You ought to have come yesterday, at the time of your appointment.'

'My appointment?!' I knew nothing about this appointment until this morning. Moreover, don't you know where I am? I'm in the prison! How could I come to you except by means of the police?'

'I have nothing to do with the police,' he replied. 'It was imperative that you be here yesterday. Anyway, we will begin investigating your case now.'

Could I possibly have any confidence in this man's sense of justice? And if he had begun with these illogical words, could there possibly be any logic or intelligence in him?

'The investigation will not take place unless my lawyer is here.'

'You have a lawyer?'

'Yes.'

He rang a bell. When an office boy came in, he said, 'Bring in Dr Nawal el Sa'adawi's lawyer.'

'Yes, sir.'

He shut the door tightly. 'We will wait a few minutes until the lawyer arrives.'

'Where will he come from?'

'From the bottom floor where the lawyers wait.'

'Did you inform the lawyer of the scheduled time of my investigation?'

'We don't inform the lawyers.'

'Why not?'

'It's not our job.'

'Whose job is it?'

'Every individual under accusation informs his own lawyer.'

'But I'm in prison and no one told me the time appointed for the session. And I have no way of contacting the lawyer, so how can I inform him?'

'That is not my concern.'

'Whose is it, then?'

'I don't know.'

'Let's suppose the lawyer didn't come today.'

'You can postpone the session to another day.'

'But postponing it means postponing the time when the true facts will appear, and therefore postponing the day I'll leave prison.'

'All right, then, you can choose not to postpone the investigation.'

'But I want the lawyer with me during the investigation. It's my right.'

'Yes, it's your right and you can postpone the session.'

'If the session is postponed, how do I guarantee that he will know of the new time, and who will inform him of this appointment?'

He remained silent, confused, not knowing what to reply. The anger was accumulating inside me . . . I wanted to explode in the face of this man whom I had imagined to represent justice, and here he was, incapable not only of justice but also of logic itself. He was avoiding my gaze.

The door opened and I saw the lawyer come in. I almost flung my arms around him, and I called out in a tone of joy, 'It's my good luck that you came today!'

'I come every day and wait with the other lawyers,' the lawyer said. 'The minute I heard the bailiff call out your name, I came at once.'

'Let's begin the investigation,' said the investigator.

'Before I start,' I said, 'I want to note for the record how the policemen invaded my home, broke down the door, searched the flat and took me to prison without having any official warrant from the Chief Prosecutor in their possession. I also want to note for the record that they put me, with my comrades, the other women who were detailed, in the beggars' cell in the Barrages Prison. Two of my cellmates came down with scabies. Our physical and mental health is threatened. We do not receive any of the rights of a defendant who is under investigation. We don't even get out into the prison courtyard, and no one visits us. We live in complete isolation behind two steel doors.'

'Doctor,' interposed the lawyer with a smile, 'I see no benefit in saying any of this.'

'No benefit?' I asked, astonished. 'How can you say that? Everything that has occurred is contrary to the law.'

The lawyer smiled again. 'Yes, that's right, and that's why there is no use in recording anything. No one will read these words. What's important is that you answer the questions concisely. There's no reason to elaborate on anything.'

'But I would like what I've said to be put on record.'

'Never mind, it's all right,' said the investigator. 'Get it all down,' he said to the clerk.

The clerk for the session began writing in his book. First, he rolled up his sleeves the better to grasp his pen. He raised one forearm in the air and brought it down over the register. This book had an amazing shape, for it resembled a record book that I'd seen in a museum in Zanzibar, dating from the days when there were slaves.

My eyes widened in perplexity. Where am I? In what age do I live? The dossier shines on the desk surface, which reflects the investigator's face and my three names on the dossier cover . . . the name of my paternal grandfather still adheres to mine. He died before I ever saw him and lived urinating blood. The investigator's head shakes above the blue dossier. He opens it . . . shuts it. Opens the official envelope with the red seal. A jagged red circle stuck on to the tip of the folded envelope flap, which was shaking under his hand with the shaking of his head.

He stares at the papers for a long time. He fishes through the dossier, his eyes searching for something, narrowing, widening. He closes one eye and opens the other . . . as if looking through a microscope. He lifts his head momentarily and then returns to the search.

The crystalline surface of the desk reflects his face in a peculiar fashion. His nose has elongated like an elephant's trunk. His eyes are small, like the eyes of needles. His fingers on the white paper in the dossier are like long needles extended inside a white body.

He is still silent. He moves his fingers along, and searches.

For what is he searching?

I recalled the inquisition trials of the Middle Ages, and the long needle which they used to plunge into the body of the woman healer/magician, searching for the mark of the devil.

Finally, he lifted his head. His eyes were wandering, far from mine. His lips parted and I heard him speak in a faint voice which sounded more like a hiss.

'The Internal Security police say that in 1972 you gave a lecture in the College of Medicine of Ain Shams University, accompanied by your ex-communist husband. In it, they say, you attacked the ruling system and incited the students to rebellion and revolution. What do you have to say to that?'

I almost burst out laughing, but I limited myself to a calm smile. 'Why don't we begin with my childhood rather than just in 1972?'

His eyes dilated in surprise. 'What did you say? I did not hear you properly.'

'For this investigation, do you draw your information about me from the Internal Security police?'

'I would like to remind you that I am the one who asks the questions, and you are to answer them, not the reverse – since I am the investigator . . . I am the judge.'

'You are the judge?!! But your title is "prosecutor". How can you be a judge and a prosecutor at the same time?'

'I've already told you that it is I who puts the questions and not you. Right. What do you think about what I said to you?'

'You mean, about what the Internal Security police said to you? Except for the fact tht I gave a lecture in the College of Medicine at Ain Shams in 1972, it is a total lie. The lecture was on the topic of

"Women and Society", and my husband was not with me.'

'The Internal Security police say that your husband was with you.'

Annoyed, I said, 'The Internal Security police are lying. They are trying to force my husband's name into it when they know perfectly well that my husband was not with me and did not attend that lecture. A professor from the university of Ain Shams was with me. A few days after the lecture, Mr Safwat Abbas asked me to come to the Bureau of State Security in Zaki Street. He asked me some questions, and then I went home. The professor who participated with me in the lecture and discussion was also asked to go to the Bureau of State Security, and was asked a few questions. That was the end of that. Nearly ten years have passed since that lecture, which was an academic, scientific lecture within the university. It must have been put on record. Also, the Internal Security police must have scrutinized my answers to the questions put by Safwat Abbas in State Security. So why distort the facts?'

'Please, I'm the one who asks the questions.'

'But I want to understand why the Internal Security police are lying, as well.'

'I have nothing to do with the Internal Security police. I represent the apparatus of the Socialist Prosecutor, which is independent of the Internal Security police.'

'If the Socialist Prosecutor apparatus is separate from the Internal Security police, why do you depend in your investigation on information which has come to you from the Internal Security police?'

The lawyer interrupted. 'Doctor, please, remember the nature of this investigation and try to respond to the questions without digressing on to other matters. You understand what I am saying.' He smiled meaningfully at me.

I smiled back at him. 'I understand, but I cannot suspend my intelligence or cancel simple logic.'

Then the second question came out, more amazing than the first one had been. 'The Internal Security police say you have Marxist leanings,' said the investigator abruptly.

This time, I did laugh. 'How do these Internal Security people find out about such leanings? I am a psychiatrist, and I know that "leanings" are merely feelings. Have the Internal Security police made an incision into my heart and found out my feelings and "leanings"? Moreover, according to whom does one enter prison because one has philosophical tendencies, Marxist or otherwise? The Egyptian constitution places no shackles on an Egyptian's "leanings", and it is the right of any individual to lean towards, become fond of, and love passionately whatever ideas and philosophies he wants.'

The lawyer laughed. 'Doctor, we all know that. The question is in error from the legal and constitutional point of view, but this investigation is something else altogether.' The lawyer turned toward the investigator. 'The doctor is a writer, with published works. All of her ideas can be found in her writings. She has not joined any political party. She is an independent personality, a novelist and fighter for the liberation of women. I suggest, with the doctor's permission, that we reduce the answer to the last question to a single word: "No."'

'This investigation does not aim to get at the truth,' the lawyer whispered into my ear. 'Rather, it aims to fish for any word which can be used against you. We don't want to give them that opportunity.'

The questions continued on in this bizarre fashion. From an envelope, the investigator drew out an issue of *Al Taqqadum* (Progress) Magazine, a periodical for public consumption published openly by the Tagammua (National Progressive Union) Party, one of Egypt's officially recognised political parties.

'They came across this magazine in your house, during the search.'

I was astonished. 'Is it a secret pamphlet? It's the organ of one of the official parties in Egypt.' The investigator indicated the first article in the magazine, which was by Khalid Muhi al-Din, Chairperson of the Tagammua Party. 'Have you read this article?'

'No.'

'Read it, and tell me what you think of it.'

My eyes widened in astonishment. 'I did not write this article. I don't understand why you want my opinion of it.'

'Do you agree with what it says?'

'I don't know what it says,' I replied, angrily this time. 'I don't know why you are asking me these peculiar questions about an article which I didn't even write. Why don't you put these questions to the author himself? Have you put me in prison and brought me here for an investigation on the basis of an article which I did not write while the author of that article is completely at liberty, sitting in his home, and no one is asking him about his article? Why don't you go to him and ask him? Why are you asking me? Am I his official agent? Am I responsible for his writings?'

The investigator lowered his head, embarrassed. Silently, he looked through the folder before him, in confusion, before pulling out another question for me – just like a magician extracting something from his bag.

'The Internal Security police say that you attacked the Camp David Treaty during the International Women's Conference held in Copenhagen in July 1980.'

'That's also a lie. The Camp David Treaty was not a topic of discussion at the conference. I was invited in one of the meetings to speak about the problems faced by Palestinian women in the occupied territories, in my capacity as the one in charge of the Women's Programme in the United Nations Economic Committee for West Asia. The lecture hall was full of journalists from all over the world, Israeli journalists included. One of the Israeli journalists got worked up after I talked about the birth of the Israeli state, from a historical perspective, and how the patriarchal and class structure had led first to the institution of slavery, then to the feudal system and then to the capitalist one, and how imperialism played a role in the founding of Israel.

'This Israeli journalist tried to interrupt me, and to create chaos in the meeting, so they threw him out of the hall. Another Israeli journalist who was there asked me: "In your capacity as a member of the U.N. Economic Committee for West Asia, can you explain to us why Israel is not one of the member states in this committee? After all, it includes the Arab nations of the region. Isn't Israel one of the region's legitimate states?"

"Why don't you go and ask the United Nations?" I replied.

"What is your personal view of this unjust situation?" the Israeli journalist asked me.

"The emergence of Israel was unjust. The state of Israel came about through the force of arms and murder in order to annihilate the Palestinian people, men and women. My personal opinion is that I see no justice in its inclusion as a United Nations state of that region."

'The meeting ended, and no one had asked me any questions about Camp David.'

'But the Internal Security police say that you attacked the Camp David Treaty in this conference,' said the investigator.

'Which Internal Security police?' I asked. 'Egyptian or Israeli?'

'Egyptian, of course.'

'If the Egyptian Internal Security police were present at that conference, then they must know what I said. My remarks at that meeting took the side of the Arab peoples and the Egyptian people against the Israeli state. What could anger the Egyptian Internal Security police about that? It is known that I do not agree with Sadat's policies, Camp David among them. I am not hiding anything, and all of my views have been published. But in this conference, specifically, no one asked me about Camp David. Why are you twisting the facts and insisting on bringing Camp David falsely into this conference?'

The investigator, maintaining silence, peered into the dossier.

I asked myself whether my name had joined the list of those under precautionary detention for precisely this reason. I was searching for a convincing explanation for my own imprisonment, and the detention of such a large number of individuals of different orientations, movements, and ideas. There was nothing in common among those whom Sadat had imprisoned except their opposition to the peace agreement with Israel.

Is Israel the reason for our presence in prison? Had it wanted to suppress the voices which oppose the Israeli cultural and economic assault that has taken place under cover of the label 'normalisation of relations'? What sort of deception has been taking place behind the screen of National Unity, Social Peace, Protecting Egypt from the Sectarian Rift and Protecting the Values of the Village from Shame?

I heard the investigator repeat himself. 'But the Internal Security police say you attacked the Camp David Treaty in the Copenhagen conference.'

I laughed. I don't know why I laughed, but I did recall a grey-haired Egyptian woman who had been in the entourage of Sadat's wife at the Copenhagen conference. She had confronted me face to face in a wide gallery and had shouted at me in an annoyed tone of voice.

'What did you say in the meeting to stir up the Israeli journalist so much that he was thrown out of the hall?'

'Since when do you defend Israel?'

Her eyes started in surprise. Her lips opened to answer me but she noticed Sadat's wife appearing at a distance and scurried away from me, speaking in a tone of alarm. 'I don't want her to see me with you.' Teetering on her spike heels, she ran toward Sadat's wife.

'Did the wife of Sadat denounce me when she returned to Egypt after the Copenhagen conference?' I asked. The investigator made no response to my question, and went on staring into the folder.

'I want to know why I am in prison,' I said angrily. 'Why was I incarcerated at the same time that Sadat was announcing the closure of all places of detention, and also cancellation of the Emergency Laws, on 15 May 1980?'

The lawyer smiled. 'On the same day, though, he issued Law No. 95 for the Protection of Values from Shame.'

'The Emergency Law was preferable,' I replied. 'At least it was a temporary law. However long martial law may be extended, it ends when the exceptional circumstances which brought about its imposition have ended. Sadat, though, wanted to establish the despotism permanently rather than temporarily, so he has issued perpetual laws to maintain oppression and he has given them innocent titles which are in contradiction with their actual nature. The Law of Values is no more than an abuse and desecration of true human values.'

The investigator continued to stare into the dossier as if he did not hear me.

He took from the folder a page from *Al Watan* (The Nation) Newspaper, which is published in Kuwait. On it, I saw my picture and an article entitled 'It is the People Who Form the Parties and not the Ruler'.

'You are the author of this article.'

'This article was published in Cairo, in *Al Shaab* Newspaper on 9 November 1981, under the title "It is the People Who Form the Parties". Do you have a copy of *Al Shaab* with you?'

'No.'

'This article is taken directly from *Al Shaab*.'

'Can you read the article carefully and confirm that you are the author of every word of it.'

I finished reading the article. At some point, I forgot that I was the author, and I was filled with admiration for whoever had written it. Suddenly, I remembered that I was the author, and the thought filled me with pride and self-admiration. The lawyer noticed my smile of satisfaction, and he smiled too. I heard the investigator speak.

'Did you write this article?'

'Yes.'

'Every letter in it?'

'Every letter.'

'And what do you think of it? Do you agree with what is said in it?'

'Completely.'

The discussion began . . . from the first paragraph of the article to the last one. The investigator read each paragraph and asked me its meaning, and then he moved on to the next one. He paused for a long time at the following passage: 'The phenomenon which we perceive today is that it is the rulers who form the political parties, or who say that they are the ones who have originated these parties, but is this in accord with the Constitution?'

'What do you mean by this sentence?' asked the investigator. 'And who are the rulers who have formed the political parties or have said that it was they who originated the parties?'

'Yes, this has occurred in Egypt,' I said. 'In the newspapers, Sadat explained that it was he who had founded the opposition parties and that if it had not been for him, they would not have come about. He said also that he was as able to crush them as he had been able to bring them into existence. Sadat used these very expressions to explain his point of view in his most recent clash with the opposition parties.'

'Yes, we've all read that in the newspapers over the recent

period,' said the lawyer.

The investigation took several hours, and encompassed questions similar to the above which I no longer remember due to their trivial nature. However, the investigator did not ask me a single question about my role in the sectarian rift, or about my participation in any foreign blueprint to create chaos in the country or to mount a coup d'état.

The Internal Security police had not been able to drum up for me the likes of those charges which the newspapers had announced and which the Consultative Council had confirmed. It became clear to me, and to the investigator, and to the lawyer, that there was nothing whatsoever against me and that my answers were all logical and convincing, while the questions were all illogical and trumped up in a laughable way.

I lifted my head proudly, feeling that truth and right were on my side. I imagined that the investigator would order my release, on the basis of my innocence. I got to my feet. 'I'll go on home now, since there is nothing against me.'

The lawyer smiled. 'Not so fast, doctor.'

'So far, I've spent 22 days in prison,' I replied angrily, 'in circumstances which are totally illegal, and without an investigation. And now, see? The investigation has uncovered nothing against me!'

'The investigation is not over yet,' said the investigator. 'We will send for you again if we obtain any new information.'

'Why should I sit in prison for that entire period? This is against the law. I should be released immediately, today. I should also be compensated for all the days I've spent in prison. When you receive new information, you can summon me from my home.'

The lawyer smiled. 'Doctor, this is an imprisonment which occurred by Sadat's order, personally, and only Sadat himself will release you when he wishes to do so!'

'This is a state without law or justice, and this investigation is absolutely useless and totally unjust.'

The investigator rang the bell, and the door opened. The officer and guards surrounded me and, once again, carried me off in the vans to prison.

On the return trip, I was sad. Beneath my feelings of grief, though, were other emotions – a sort of odd desire for my cellmates, as if I had been absent for years rather than hours, and a sort of delight because I was returning to them. I was amazed by these sensations. I was discovering, though, that prison life creates a sort of unique comradeship among those imprisoned. Instantly, I imagined that I was returning to my own folk, to my warm family in that isolated cell at the end of the world.

As soon as the van approached the Barrages the faces of my cellmates came back to me – their eyes at night as they searched for my eyes, their voices calling mine, our mutual assistance and support in confronting the prison administration, sitting together in the dirt enclosure picking the impurities out of *ful*-beans and lentils. Sometimes, our happy laughter. Indeed, from a distance even the differences and quarrels appeared dear to me.

But the huge prison doors sparked off a shivering through my body. There it all was – the small gap in which my body bent double in order to pass through, the *shawisha*'s fingers and hands passing over my head and body as she searched me, the steel doors, the voices, the odour, and the heavy, stagnant air pressing on my chest and heart.

No sooner did the door to the cell open, though, than the eyes inside dilated in joy and surprise, and the friendly, warm voices rose, calling out to me in pleasure. 'We've missed you . . . it's as if you've been away for an entire year, rather than just one day!'

Eagerly, they gathered to sit around me, asking what had happened during the investigation. I told them the story just as it had happened, in complete detail. I acted out some of the gestures of the officers and the detained fellow prisoners in the waiting room. I told them that the prosecutor's fingers inside the dossier were like needles used in the courts of the Inquisition, searching for the mark of the devil. We laughed until we almost passed out. I was like the narrator of a farce or a comedy from the theatre of the absurd; the laughs reverberated in the cell. But it was only moments before uneasy silence returned to us . . . and sadness. 'There's no hope to be had for the investigation or in justice, or in anything,' remarked one cellmate. 'I've said so hundreds of times.'

'There's no hope except in God's justice,' another replied. And a despondent silence crept over us, long as the entire night.

In the middle of the night, I heard a voice moaning faintly. I saw Itidaal lying on her bed with her eyes open. Tears covered her face. Her lips were parted as if murmuring verses from the Qur'an. Boduur was by her side, patting her shoulder and reciting verses to her.

'Is she sick?' I whispered.

'No. She went out for an investigation session and came back in this state.'

I placed my hand on her forehead. It was hot, inflamed, as if she'd come down with a fever. Her body was shivering, and her face was pale. I stripped the blanket from my bed, covered her, and took hold of her wrist to count the pulse. Her eyes caught mine and her lips parted to let out a faint, broken voice, sounding like interrupted breathing or the delirium of a feverish person.

'My mother wasn't there, she must be ill, she didn't come with my aunt to the session. My aunt – she's my mother's sister – has been going to the prosecutor's office every day. Going every day, in order to see her son and to see me. She didn't have a lawyer with her, and me, I don't know anything. I cried, I was afraid to go in to the prosecutor by myself. I saw my cousin in handcuffs. My aunt said that a lawyer costs money, and she doesn't have any. She said people told her that a lawyer isn't of any use anyway. The charges are serious, and people told her the problem is a hard one, hardest thing in the world, and no lawyer can solve it. And there are lots of charges, and lots of people charged, and lots of orders, ones that people know about and ones which aren't known, that need a lot of digging to get out. They keep all of the orders, the publicly known ones and the unknown ones, in a large building. The lawyer has to go there himself. There are lots of offices and lots of floors, too many to count. If he is able to know the way and to reach the right door he has to leave his identity card at the entrance and wait in a room with the other lawyers. The lawyers' room is on the bottom floor next to the toilet. My aunt saw them there with her own eyes because she tried to go to the toilet. They kept her from going in and told her it was the buffet. She saw the lawyers crammed into the room like sardines, maybe a hundred, or a thousand, no one knows. On top of each other . . . standing up all day and waiting, just like the beggars in front of Sayyida Zaynab mosque. People told my aunt that they were waiting for an official pass from the Presiding Judge of the Grand Court, and my aunt asked what the name of the court was. No one knew any name for the court or any name for the Presiding Judge. But they told her that the pass was crucial. The lawyer can't do anything without the pass, and he can't get it in one day, either. The matter takes a long time, because the Presiding Judge doesn't come in every day, since he has other business in lots of offices on lots of floors, and all the orders are with him, in his desk drawer. No one has the key to the drawer except him, personally. When he travels, he takes the key with him. If he is away for a month or two, no one can open the drawer. People told my aunt that the orders are secret and have secret numbers. But every order has a number in series. As long as the number is in series, it has a date – day and hour. And the lawyer has to know the number and the date. Without the number and the date, he can't get the order. But as long as the numbers are in series, the order has to show up, out in the open, sometime, even if it takes a year. The important thing, though, is that the lawyer has to know the way to it, or he must know someone who knows the Presiding Judge, or the Deputy, or the secretary, or even the office boy. My aunt had got to know the office boy. She said he's the most important one because he is the first one to know if the Presiding Judge is there or not, if he's away travelling or not. The proper lawyer, though, one who has a conscience, has to get results, because God is with those who are proper and virtuous. My aunt knows a lawyer who has a conscience, but she says that he's a green young man and doesn't know anyone. He asked her for 30 pounds down payment, and my aunt only had ten with her. Since he has a conscience, he told her the facts frankly and refused to take the ten pounds. He told her: "Put the money back in your pocket, Hagga, I can't be of any use nor can any lawyer. There's no point in obtaining the number of the order or even the order itself – because it isn't a question of the order, or of a number, or anything. The problem is a big and difficult one and it can't be solved by a lawyer or a judge. No one but God – His Might be praised – can solve it.'

'My aunt wrung her hands, and asked him, "What shall I do, Sir?" "Perform you ablutions and pray to God, Hagga," he told her. I saw my aunt crying, and I started crying like her. I went into the prosecutor by myself, shaking with fear. He asked me, "What's your name, you there, clever girl?" "My name's Itidaal," I said. "And what are the names of your father and grandfather?" I told him all the names, even the names of my mother and aunt. He wrote it all down on a piece of paper and asked, "Where are you at the moment, Itidaal?" "In the Barrages Prison, in the political women's cell," I told him. "Who is with you in the cell, Itidaal?" he asked me. I said, "Good people are with me" "Like whom, Itidaal?" "A doctor whose name is Nawal el Sa'adawi," I told him. "Nawal el Sa'adawi is with you?" he said. "Watch out for her!" "Why should I?" I asked. "Watch out for what she tells you – she might put you under a spell with her words and turn your mind upside down." "She's a good lady," I told him, "and she has good things to say, and we're all good together, we're getting on really well there." He told me, "All right, go on along now, Itidaal." "I can go home now?" I asked. "I mean, go on back to prison now," he said, "and tomorrow you'll have another session here with me." "All right," I said, "But why tomorrow? Why don't you ask me everything today so I can be done with it, and forget about coming again tomorrow?" He said, "I have lots of other people to see today and tomorrow God willing you'll come along here again, Itidaal." "How will I come?" He said, "They know, and they'll bring you, don't you worry about a thing now." '

Part V
The Death of Sadat

The investigative session dissipated the final glimmer of hope that justice might exist. It confirmed that there was no law, no jurisprudence, and no justice. As for this apparatus called the Public Prosecutor, or the Socialist Public Prosecutor, it was no more than an instrument to cancel the law, efface one's rights and the truth, and erase the facts. Where was the Egyptian judiciary system? Where were the courts?

I began to sense the weight of imprisonment. Around me, my cellmates were mute and sad. The secret of the Public Prosecutor had been revealed: there was no hope of release as long as Sadat was in power. How long would he remain so?

Whenever our grief and misery grew to excruciating proportions, we believed that he would remain in power forever. Surely we would die in prison and he buried beneath the wall. All the while, Sadat would continue to grip absolute power with both hands.

Whenever our imaginations ran wild, we fancied that he had been afflicted with an incurable disease or a sudden paralysis, which would prevent him from continuing to hold power.

If we were struck by a mad bout of hope, our dreams would produce a coup in the army which would remove him from power as had happened to King Farouq. Neither consciously nor unconsciously could we conceive of anything beyond these possibilities.

His death was not a notion which occurred to any intellect or imagination, awake or asleep. We heard that he took good care of his health – sleeping a lot, working little, running in the open air, eating healthy food, not devoting much energy to thought. Those who think die early, while those who avoid thought remain physically strong. His death was a stroke of the impossible of which we did not even permit ourselves to dream. Dreams such as this might weaken one, and by instinct alone we stayed far away from dreams which held little promise of realisation.

Then that day came . . . We were sitting on the ground, our backs to the wall . . . Our hearts were heavy, our eyes inflamed with the dust, our faces stained with the black soot of the chimney. Our feet, peeking out from plastic slippers, were cracked and split. Our *gallabiyyas*, covered in spots of every hue, were soiled with dirt. Our hair was mussed. We sat behind the bars like animals imprisoned inside steel cages.

I raised my eyes and my lips parted to say something. I shut them tightly, though. What did I have to say when the last flicker of hope had been extinguished?

Suddenly, we saw Dhuba opening the door and coming into our area, panting for breath. Her brown face was glowing with a reddish gleam and her eyes were like two live coals. She called out, her voice breathless, 'Have you heard the news?'

'What news?'

'Sadat – they've shot him!'

The movement of her lips as she pronounced the words appeared to me like a movement from beyond this universe. The entire moment was outside our universe. The earth whirled round, and the brown lips revolved like the earth rotating. Dhuba's face became two lips the size of the globe, revolving and repeating, 'They shot him . . .'

I was not the only one to experience such a sensation. I saw all of the faces around me pumped full of blood, eyes dilated, hands grabbing Dhuba – her arms, her legs, her head – and shaking her, jolting her, making sure that she was awake and in her right mind, that she was not raving as she repeated 'They've shot him . . . they've shot him . . . they've . . .'

Hysteria inundated the cell: bodies flinging themselves on Dhuba unawares, hugging and kissing her. Dhuba throttled by hugs and kisses, pulling herself from beneath the bodies. She was still breathing 'they've shot him . . .'

Everyone breathes the question in unison: 'And he died?'

'I don't know' moans Dhuba.

Facial muscles freeze. The sinews of the tongue congeal. Chest

muscles stop in place, and the air ceases to move. Chests are
motionless. Tongue frozen in throat. The word gets stuck in the
throat.

'He didn't die?'

Still groaning, Dhuba replies. 'Don't know.'

Eyes bulge, rotate, like pendulums, astray, bewildered, terrified
as the sudden wild hope fades like a mirage. Chests, swollen with
hope to the point of bursting, contract and drop to the pits of
despair and wretchedness.

'If he's alive . . .' someone shrieked . . .

'. . . he'll spare no one,' we all moaned. 'We'll all be butchered
. . . he'll take his revenge on *us* . . .'

Bodies toppling one upon another, on to Dhuba who is still
pulling herself out from among them, groaning, 'If the Internal
Security officer were to arrive right now . . .'

They scattered themselves at a distance from her, everyone
panting hard with this overwhelming sensation. They tried to
master it, tightening lip muscles to close their mouths, to suppress
their voices. 'Tell us, Dhuba,' someone whispered. 'How did you
find out the news? Who shot him, and where, and when?'

Dhuba straightened her hair, which had become dishevelled in
the fray, and arranged her *gallabiyya*, which had slipped under the
grasping hands and arms, as if she had just disentangled herself
from a physical struggle. She moistened her lips. 'I heard the news
just now on the telly. We were in the cell, and all of us were
watching the military show, and suddenly we heard shots, and the
dispatch stopped . . . and we heard someone say that they'd shot
Sadat and taken him to the hospital.'

It was early afternoon, nearly two o'clock. We still had two hours
to get through before the four o'clock closing time. We had never
taken the transistor radio from its hiding place in the ground before
closing time, when the two steel doors were locked upon us, the
shawisha returned to her home, and the whole prison administration staff were on the way home.

'We've got to get out the radio and follow the news,' I said.

'Let's get it out,' they echoed in unison.

Even Fawqiyya, the most cautious of any of us, jumped up to
extract the radio from its hiding spot. Boduur, who had considered

the radio a satanic implement which paved the road to hell because it broadcast profligate songs, called out 'Let's listen to the radio!'

We got out the magic instrument which was as small as the palm of a hand. I took hold of it, enveloping it in my palm, my heart thumping. I placed it over my ear. I could hear only the pounding of my heart and the hearts of my cellmates, as they drew their heads close to mine, placing their ears as near as possible to that little object the size of a cigarette packet.

The magic voice came out. 'This is Cairo . . .'

Hearts stopped beating. Breathing ceased. We imagined that he would announce news of the death . . . and a long, heavy silence descended . . . no sound, no movement, chests motionless, breathing utterly cut off.

Without warning, the voice of a female singer pealed from the radio. The blood coagulated in our veins. Fawqiyya shrieked, slapping her cheeks, 'He's been rescued from death!' The others moaned, lips dry. 'Catastrophe . . .'

The singer's voice grew louder, sounding throughout the cell. Gazing at the door, Dhuba shrieked. 'The *shawisha* has arrived, folks! Hide the radio!'

The radio was in my hand. I muffled it and hurried to the toilet, disappearing inside. From behind the door left ajar, I heard the *shawisha*'s voice addressing Dhuba: 'What are you doing here, girl? Hmm, Dhuba? You haven't cleaned out the cell or swept the enclosure. Go on now, go back to your own cell, right now! I don't want to see your face in here.'

Her voice sounded unsettled; it was hiding something. She must have heard the news, and wanted to prevent it from seeping in to us.

All was silence in the cell – a quiet which was shattered by Fawqiyya's voice, calm and empty of emotion, as it was on any other day. 'Any news, *shawisha*? Has anything new happened lately?'

The *shawisha*'s voice sounded just as even and unagitated as it always did, too, lacking any sort of new excitement. 'Not at all . . . no news whatsoever . . . nothing new under the sun.'

Her words reached me as I stood in the lavatory, unable to see her eyes. There was a slight vacillation in her voice, a tremor so concealed that it would not be perceived by an ordinary ear. It was a voice trained to hide the facts.

I waited until I heard a cellmate's voice calling from behind the broken half door. 'The *shawisha* has gone away.'

'She might come in again,' I replied. 'Or the Internal Security officer might show up. I'll stay here, behind the door, monitoring the news on the radio. If you notice anyone coming in from the courtyard, tell me right away.'

'I'll watch the door to the enclosure,' she said. 'Don't turn up the radio. Leave it against your ear.'

'It's there.'

'If I see anyone coming, I'll call out "O God of the heavens, *ya ilah assamawaat*". That's the signal – "O God of the heavens".'

The lavatory was cramped and stifling. I supported my back against the wall. Before my face was the broken half door. If I moved an arm, my elbow would strike the wall to my right or left. The toilet hole, full of excrement and stinking water, occupied half the space of the lavatory – I could not stand without having it between my feet.

For three hours, I stood in that position, like one crucified, with one arm lifted next to my head, holding that square metal object jammed against my ear. My other arm was raised, too, fingers moving the revolving dial . . . This is London . . . This is Cairo . . . Voice of America . . . Monte Carlo . . . voices speaking in every language. I heard a voice saying, 'It's a light wound, nothing serious, just one in the arm.'

The earth spun round. The walls of the lavatory closed in upon me. I stopped breathing. The sweat poured from my head and arms and legs, and my *gallabiyya* clung to my body.

I opened the door quickly, afraid of suffocating. My cellmates gathered around me. In a feeble, despairing voice, I said, 'It's a light wound, in the arm.'

Bodies dropped to the ground, some swooning, some in a near coma. I mastered my feelings of despair, pulled myself from the ground and moved my paralysed legs. 'I'll keep on following the news. Maybe this is a false report. They're resisting the sudden confusion which his death might cause. Maybe they're concealing the news of his death until they can get over the shock and prepare to defend their rights in the Middle East without him.'

I went back to my place in the toilet enclosure. I stiffened myself between the wall and the door, the stinking hole between my feet. The wound was still minor . . . but the voice of the announcer bore a hesitation, the tremor of a voice which is concealing the truth. I heard a cellmate calling out '*Ya ilah assamawaat*'. I remembered the signal, pressed my hand on the dial, and cut off the voice. I heard the *shawisha*'s voice in the enclosure.

'Good night, ladies. Sleep well.'

'Good night, *shawisha*, Sleep well.'

The key turned in the door to the cell three times. I waited until I heard the key turn three times in the door to the enclosure, and then I bounded out of the lavatory. I sat down on my bed, surrounded by my cellmates. Our heads were pressed against each other, our ears as near as possible to those tiny holes, so like the puncture marks made by a needle, in that metal object the size of one's palm. Our breaths came in close succession, our heads crowded together . . . and we heard the voice: 'This is London . . .'

Silence fell; we held our breaths. The implacable voice came. 'We have received confirmation that Sadat has died.'

The bodies exploded into the air, as the radio fell to the ground. No one paid any attention to it. This was a moment outside of time, outside of the universe, impossible to touch with the senses. Perhaps we'd lost our five senses and could no longer see or hear anything. Around me, objects were whirling round. I grasped my head. Was this a dream or was it certain, scientifically verifiable knowledge? What was this revolving around me? The earth? The cell? Or was it me that was revolving?

I became aware, suddenly, of a strange scene: Boduur whirling around, minus *niqaab* and cloak, whirling and dancing, surrounded by her cellmates who usually wore *niqaabs*, dancing with hair uncovered, without face-veils or head-coverings, bodies rocking violently, waists bending, bellies quivering, heads swaying, hair flying.

And another bizarre scene: Fawqiyya, who had never in her life performed a single ritual prayer sequence, was kneeling on the ground, raising her hands to the sky and shouting, "I give praise to You, O Lord.' Around her, the other cellmates were kneeling, praying, calling out in unison, 'O Lord, we give praise to Thee.'

My attention was drawn from the dancing and the praying by something even odder: the attempt to keep the moment in my grip. I feared it would slip away, that I would open my eyes and know that it had been a dream. I gazed at the walls and bars of the prison and said 'It is not a dream. The fact that I am in prison proves it.'

Fawqiyya called out in a hysterical voice, imitating Sadat's oratorical tone: 'I will have no mercy . . .' and Boduur shouted, 'Glory be to You, O Lord.'

I was still incapable of hanging on to that moment. My rational mind understood the truth. My heart was about to burst with joy and hope. But a cell in my brain remained anxious and apprehensive. We were still behind bars. Who had killed Sadat? And what would happen now? Anything might occur. A coup, perhaps . . . a revolution . . . we might be released, or we might be slaughtered inside the prisons. As long as a bullet had been released which had killed the President of the Republic as he was surrounded by guards, policemen, and soldiers, everything was possible and anything was likely to happen.

Who had fired that bullet? And how?

For the first time in Egypt's history, a bullet is shot and kills the President of the Republic. Through what historical moment was I living, mind and body, as I sat inside this prison?

'Whomsoever kills is killed,' Boduur called. 'Though it be long after.'

My heart pounds beneath my ribs. Joy mingles with anxiety, facts of the matter are blended with my imagination. My eyes follow the dancing and the kneeling in prayer, and move from the ceiling to the walls. From afar, the face of my husband appears to me, and those of my daughter, and son . . . they must have heard the news. What are they doing right now?

The dream began to loom in the distance. I threw it off momentarily and it returned to me. I saw myself in my own home. I rejected the thought . . . it came back to me and I pushed it away once again. Breaths coming in rapid succession . . . my chest heaving . . . blood rushing to my head . . . a vessel in my brain about to burst.

I rose quickly. 'Even if we don't get out of here, friends, the country has been liberated.' We all called out in unison, 'Yes, the country has been liberated!'

Not one of us closed an eye that night. The blood pumping through the arteries of our brains repelled sleep. Dreams and hopes crept in to scatter the gloom of night. We heard drums and dancing emerging from the other cells. The voice of the *shawisha* was was on night duty rang out in the evening air, speaking to us through the bars. 'Congratulations, political women . . . congratulations and, God willing, you've all been freed, and the whole country has been freed, God willing.'

Voices in the prison reverberated, singing a well-known political song:

Who are they, who are they,
Egyptian soldiers, hurray hurray!
Who are they, who are they,
Our nationalist boys, hurray, hurray!

Boduur called out, 'It's the feast day tomorrow, friends! The Great Feast.' Voices burst out singing a traditional feastday song:

O eve of the feast,
Your presence has honoured us.
You've renewed the hope within us,
O eve of the feast.

In the morning, we took our seats as usual. We hid the radio in the ground, and put the masks over our faces to make it appear that we knew nothing of the news, that we were still living in the age of Sadat. Sadness was sketched on our faces . . . and despair.

The prison administration, in complete array, came in. Some were wearing black neckties. Their faces looked pale, and their eyes were red. Like us, they must not have slept at all the previous night.

Worry runs through those eyes like mercury. They don't know what is going to happen. They have orders to conceal the news of the death from those detained here.

'Today is the Feast,' Boduur said in a barely-heard voice. 'Happy Feast Day, and many happy returns.'

'We want to buy meat for the feast,' one of the *munaqqabas* said. 'Everyone will be eating meat during the feast except us.'

'We will buy meat for you,' said the chief prison official. 'You have money in the prison safe.'

'No!' called Boduur. 'We do not eat meat from the market! We don't know who has slaughtered it, and whether it was slaughtered according to Muslim practice or not. We want to buy two chickens and slaughter them ourselves.'

The chief prison official smiled. 'We will buy you healthy chickens so you can slaughter them according to the Muslim way.'

I fixed my eyes on the face of the Internal Security officer. His eyes were shifting back and forth rapidly – an obvious anxiety which he was trying to hide. Beneath the cast of worry was something like a profound relaxation or a concealed joy. He opened his lips as if to present us with the news, but he retreated and closed his mouth in silence. The chief prison administrator was also hiding his happiness, but his eyes betrayed him, as they sparkled in a smile. Before he turned to leave, he said to us, 'Happy Feast Day, ladies, and many happy returns.'

As they walked away, I observed their backs. Slightly stooped, the fatigue marked upon them. Worry. Confusion. Men who had become, by virtue of their employment, prison guards or executioners or spies on other human beings. In their depths the human being still sat, latent . . . No sooner is the corrupt atmosphere transformed than the human being extends his head to look, and sniffs the aroma of the pure air.

Why had they concealed the news of the death from us? Had they received instructions from above to hide it? Or was it a question of custom, habituation, and practices acquired by those working in such jobs?

Before they were completely out of the door, I called to them, and they turned back towards me. I fixed my eyes on the eyes of the senior official among them and said, 'I want paper and a pen to write a request to Sadat.'

My voice was normal, just as if Sadat were still alive. I saw the quivering in those eyes, and the paleness in their faces. I saw the muscles just above the mouth twitch, and the lips parting in a movement closer to fear than any other emotion. I saw confusion, surprise, hesitation, and then stillness.

My narrative imagination and the artistic fiend within me record this moment, etching the image and the tragedy – the human being imprisoned inside his own fear.

They must know that we know. The whole prison knows. Every cell has a radio or a television, so how could the news fail to reach us?

It was not within their ability to hide the news for more than one day. The next day, they came in, smiling, amicable, speaking with us in a different manner and tone. One of them laughed. 'Who knows what will happen tomorrow? That's politics for you! One day in prison and the next in power!'

'And the next in the grave,' said Boduur.

Silence prevailed. No one wanted to remember the assassination incident itself. No one knows what will happen tomorrow. True, he has died, but who can guarantee that he will not wake up once again? Some people imagined him to be superhuman, living on and ruling forever after. Their eyes are still filled with fear and worry. Nothing is guaranteed. No one knows the invisible or the supernatural.

Did anyone expect that this god who had sat upon the throne and said, at the top of his voice, 'I will show no mercy' would topple over on his face and hit the ground, and that the feet (running far away from him) would trample on the cap he had been wearing, on the medals, and on the star which he had hung upon his chest?

It was on 28 September 1981 that I left the prison for my investigation before the Socialist Prosecutor, and then returned to prison. One week later, on 6 October 1981, Sadat died by the bullet. That was just one month after the date – 6 September 1981 – on which he had sent his policemen to break down the door to my home and take me off to prison.

After Sadat's death, our hope of leaving prison began once again to dance before our eyes. All of our dreams were reawakened, and with them were aroused – not surprisingly – the emotions of worry, waiting, and anticipation.

I lost all stability and calmness. I could no longer concentrate on anything. I was even incapable of writing. No sooner did I take hold of my pen than the face of my husband would flicker before me, as did those of my son and daughter. My imagination would take fire and I would fancy myself, case in hand, standing before the door to my home, ringing the doorbell . . . they would open the door . . .

Sitting down on the dirt floor, I tried to think about something else. But my brain cells were no longer capable of that. The dream which I had not permitted myself to have before Sadat's death became the sole dream which could fill my head . . . chasing out all other thoughts . . . expelling repose, repelling sleep, and rejecting calmness and stability.

I became unable to sit still, or to stand, or to remain quiet even for a few moments. My body moved automatically. I'd sit down, stand up, walk in the cell, never still. Should any voice ring out, I would turn around at once, imagining that the voice was calling to me, and that someone was telling me to pack my bag.

The days passed, however, one after another, and we heard nothing about a new order which would cancel Sadat's detention order. Inside the prison, changes began to take place. They allowed us to read the newspapers, listen to the radio, obtain food from home, and send letters to our families. The period of offence and difficulty was over, and we obtained what the other prisoners had been getting all along – except for the right to go out into the courtyard. We were also forbidden to see our families.

Every Tuesday at one p.m., though, the Internal Security officer entered, carrying a letter from my husband, followed by one of the prisoners or the *shawisha* carrying containers of food. The letter would already have been read by the Internal Security officer, who got to read it before I did. He always gave me the letter with a smile, saying, 'Dr Sherif came by, and here's his letter to you.'

The letter was open, and so were the cartons of food. Everything had to be searched carefully before it reached us. But Sherif's words on the bit of paper – points of light in the darkness – returned me to life.

Since the winter of 1964 Sherif has been part of my life. Moments of love, touches with the warmth of the sun's rays in winter, pleasurable dialogue which reaches into one's very depths. The men around him took on the appearance of idle chatterers, children, while he kept his silence. When he spoke, though, the others grew

silent. He spent thirteen years of his youth in prison. He is modest
to the point of greatness, and great to the point of modesty, strong
to the point of gentleness and lucidity, gentle to the point of
absolute unyieldingness and true strength. Rare as a pure breeze in
the Barrages Prison, or as a courageous and sincere opinion in a
debased and corrupt society. I said angrily to the Internal Security
official, 'My husband comes to the prison and I don't see him?'

'Visits are prohibited.'

'Then I'll write to him and ask him not to come. I don't want him
to come all this distance just to bring me tins of food. I don't want
food.' I wrote the letter and the Internal Security officer delivered it
to him.

But Sherif continued to come to the prison every Tuesday
without seeing me, leaving the cartons of food and the letter and
then departing calmly. I began to look forward to Tuesdays. I would
embrace the letter with my hands and eyes; I'd read it, then reread
it, close my eyes and dream that I was swimming in a sea of sunlight.

As soon as the voice of the curlew reverberated as each Tuesday
dawned, I saw the eyes sparkle and smile at me through the
eyeholes of the *niqaab*. 'It's Tuesday, Dr Nawal. Naturally, the
world isn't big enough to hold you today!' Opening their eyes, my
cellmates smiled and called out, 'Tuesday, Nawal, Tuesday!' And
through the bars, I saw the dawn light ripping apart the clouds of
night, as a fresh breeze dispelled the smoke and dust.

One day, we read in the newspapers that Hosni Mubarak had
published an order to abolish commercial announcements in the
newspapers and to stop reproducing his picture as President of the
Republic inside these announcements on special occasions and feast
days, as was customarily done. The cellmates applauded in delight.

We used to see portraits of Sadat in the commercial notices of
food security firms, other enterprises, any sort of commercial
business or shop. As a feast day drew near, merchants and owners
of firms vied to publish their greetings to Sadat and to announce
their support and loyalty.

Even the top civil servants in the central government and the
provincial governorates, as well as the presidents of organisations
and public sector officials, participated in these advertisements,

publishing photographs of Sadat beneath which ran words of fealty and support.

There were notices and portraits of Sadat everywhere – on the corner of any street, in every public square, in all commercial notices, on every page of the newspapers and magazines, on the film screen and on the television. You could not possibly raise your eyes to look at something without seeing Sadat's portrait, enlarged or reduced, smiling or stern, in army dress or naval uniform or civilian suit, or in the sash of a judge, or wearing a village cloak.

Pictures and notices cost the state millions of pounds. And every senior official in any sector must participate in the parade of advertisements, otherwise he would become a stranger to the system, not to be tolerated. Or he might be subject to persecution.

'So Hosni Mubarak is different!' called out a cellmate. 'No love lost for hypocrisy and falsehood.'

'The processions of hypocrites benefit no one,' someone else said. 'Where were they all when Sadat died?'

'They all disappeared, terrified. They left him to die alone, and to be buried alone.'

'Sadat's funeral took place without a people. A few foreigners, the presidents of Israel and the United States, marched behind him.'

'No one grieves for the deceased but his own family and those who have benefited from him.'

'Is it possible for conditions in our country to change?' I asked.

Hope was appearing on the horizon. This new president did not wish to propagandise on his own behalf through commercial announcements or Open Door firms. After all, for any ruler true propaganda consists of what he does. Is it possible that we are taking a few steps forward?

In spite of this, though, we read in the newspapers that the President of the Republic was announcing that precautionary detention was not a punishment.

We were astounded. We decided to compose a cable to him. If it was precautionary detention which we were experiencing in prison, how could it not be a punishment? During Sadat's life, we had refused to direct any request, no matter what it might be, his way. We had refused to address him or to send him any bit of paper or protest. But the new president was not the one who had imprisoned us, and we could address him. We asked for a pen and some paper, sat down on the ground, and wrote out the cable as follows:

To Mr Hosni Mubarak, President of the Republic

We have read your explanation, as published in the newspapers, that precautionary detention is not a punishment. We do not understand this expression, since imprisonment behind bars, inside a prison, is a punishment in itself. Then what is one to make of being prevented from having the legal and human rights which the accused individual under investigation is meant to enjoy? To this day, we have been denied the right to have the charges against us defined. We have not been permitted to enjoy the situation of one whose investigation has taken place. We are still barred from meeting our lawyers and families, while censorship is still imposed over correspondence with our immediate families, and we are not given any indication as to whether or not they actually receive our correspondence. We are not permitted to go out into the prison courtyard like the rest of the prisoners, or the ordinary ones. We are living in the beggars' cell, in a place saturated with smoke and dust, the fumes of burnt gas, and infection-bearing insects, which expose us to material and mental damage of the worst sorts, and which make precautionary detention not just a single punishment, but a multiple one.

We all signed the cable, submitted it to the Internal Security officer, and requested a reply.

No response reached us. We did not know whether or not the cable had arrived. When we asked the Internal Security officer about it, he said, 'I gave it to my bureau chief, and I don't know anything more about it. It must have arrived.'

Days and weeks passed. Pessimism reigned, and our hopes were dispelled. Illness began to threaten the health of some of the cellmates. One had a haemorrhage; I demanded that a gynaecologist be brought from outside the prison. We had discovered that the women's prison had no gynaecologist, male or female. Another cellmate was in her final months of pregnancy, and she began to get spells of fainting and weakness. I had started to get spinal pains due to sleeping poorly, the dampness of the ground, and the cold wind which came in at night through the bars with the end of autumn and the onset of winter.

One night, a cellmate began to shiver from the cold. Her complexion grew pale and her limbs trembled uncontrollably. 'They've got to block up the door and windows,' she said. 'I can't stay in this cell in the wintertime.'

'I'll die if I have to spend the winter here,' screamed another. The word 'death' began to echo on the cell inhabitants' tongues. The atmosphere was stifling and oppressive. The chimney smoke doubled in amount and grew in thickness and blackness. The bit of sky over the dirt enclosure turned a grey that was the colour of the dust. Dhuba became ill and no longer came to us. The *shawisha*'s steps grew slower and heavier. She had wrapped a black shawl around her head, and put her feet into thick black stockings. They took Fathiyya-the-Murderess to the workhouse.

My heart is heavy. Deep within me is a struggle against sickness, death, and pessimism. The faces around me have faded, though, and the eyes have lost the flare which signals anger, to be replaced by gazes that are dejected and submissive, as if waiting their turn to die.

We opened our eyes in the morning to find a news item in the papers. One of our detained male fellow prisoners had died in prison.

In unison, the cellmates shrieked, 'Death has arrived in the men's prison! Soon it will come over to us.'

The survival instinct was aroused. The dejected, submissive gaze vanished and I saw eyes blazing with a new flame. It was like the last moment of awareness and alertness which precedes the final breath. Human vitality before the end of human existence. Movement began to creep into our bodies – a half-crazed sort of movement, one which neither died down nor grew calmer.

A single question pierces the dormant brain cells, propelling motion into them and engendering a half-mad confusion which refuses to grow still. What are we to do? Death is approaching us – are we going to stay quiet about it? Are we going to die? The rebellious demon inside me woke up, repeating his words over and over: We will not die. If we are to die, we will not pass in the night without creating an uproar! We must rage and rage!

We gathered in a circle, our heads close together. I saw even Boduur and Fawqiyya with us inside the circle. We stood next to each other, pressed close together, one leaning on the arm of the next.

'What are we to do?'

'There are fourteen of us. Each one has two arms. That's 28 arms. If every forearm takes up some object, we might be able to batter down the door.'

Each of us went running into the cell. One stripped off an iron post from her bed. Another lifted a heavy rock which we had been using as a seat. Another grasped the wooden pestle (which we had borrowed from the murderesses' cell to pound our *ful*-beans). Still another took hold of a brass pot in which we had been cooking our lentils. Someone grabbed the metal gas burner. Whoever could find nothing else took up her aluminium plate.

We began knocking at the bars on the door, calling out all together: 'We will destroy this prison! We will not die without noise!' The steel door rocked under the heavy blows. The prison vibrated with the sound which had become like the roar of a waterfall.

From the inner selves of human beings threatened with death emerged the tyrannical demon – the latent strength long imprisoned, the stored-up energy suppressed since the remote past, since childhood, since birth, or rather from before birth, ever since those human beings were foetuses in their mothers' wombs.

The prison administrative staff hastened to us. What had happened? What had lifted the lid and revealed the rebellious demon caged inside the seashell?

A fellow prisoner of ours had died in prison and we were all threatened with death. Why were we still in prison when the President of the Republic had explained that precautionary detention is not a punishment? Why should we be punished with imprisonment when we were without crimes? Without charges? Without a fair investigation? Without learning the outcome of the investigation?

The chief prison official, the Internal Security officer, and other officials spoke with us. The Socialist Prosecutor was looking into every case, they told us, and would free any case whose innocence was established.

We replied angrily that there was nothing new in this explanation or phrasing. How long had the Socialist Prosecutor been studying the cases? And how long would those innocent ones remain behind bars? Would they be compensated for the days, weeks, and months which they had spent in prison with neither wrongdoing nor crime? 'I have no answers to these questions,' the Internal Security official said.

'Who does have the answers?' we asked.

'The Socialist Prosecutor, the Chief Attorney, and the President of the Republic.'

As always, the revolt in the cell ended with our acquisition of pen and paper. We wrote a statement addressed to the President of the Republic, the Socialist Prosecutor, and the Chief Attorney, in which we said the following:

We, the women and girls consigned to the Barrages Prison, the political prisoners specifically, announce our protest against the situation in which we find ourselves. Included among us is a mother who has been prevented from nursing her newborn, and a woman who has reached her final weeks of pregnancy without receiving any of the physical and mental care necessary to her condition. Among us are mothers who have been kept from seeing their children and husbands for month after month, and invalids who have requested examinations by specialists, to no avail. Among us are students who have been prevented from study. We are women who have been taken forcibly from our homes, and from among our families, without having committed any crime, and thrown into prison cells under the worst of human conditions, exposed to all sorts of psychological and material oppression and to grave dangers, from psychological, mental and moral damage to bodily harm, and threats to our social, professional, and family lives. To this day, we are exposed to these ills, which represent punitive measures that have been taken against us despite the numerous explanations given by the new President of the Republic to the effect that those under preventive detention are not being punished. Yet, this is an ongoing punishment in all of the forms it takes. It suffices that we are denied the right to see our children and relatives, and that we suffer from negligence, intended or not, with regard to our mental and physical health. It is this negligence which has destroyed the life of one of our fellow prisoners, and which might take the life of any one of us.

Thus, we announce our objection to the continuation of our imprisonment. We request immediate release and censure of all the kinds of mental and physical oppression and all the sorts of torture, mental and bodily, to which the political prisoner, male or female, is subjected. We request that those orders and laws which fetter one's liberties be abolished, just as we request that the campaigns of slander and falsehood which the newspapers are publishing cease.

We all signed the statement, submitted it to the Internal Security officer, and awaited the reply.

One morning – 23 November 1981 – I unfolded one of the local newspapers (*Al Ahram*) and read on the front page the names of some of the individuals who had been put under preventive detention – my name among them. I read that these individuals had been accused by the General Intelligence Bureau of implementing a Soviet blueprint in which the forces of rejection had been participating jointly to create a state of chaos in the country by trafficking in the problems of the masses, fanning the sectarian disputes, exploiting the Islamic groups, and inciting the populace to mount a revolution which would direct the country towards communism.

How could the newspaper publish this lie? The General Intelligence Bureau and the State Security Bureau had not been able to direct anything like this accusation against me personally, and among the questions which the Socialist Prosecutor had asked me, there had been no query about any such conspiracy as this.

The *shawisha* opened the door; she found me in an agitated state, irritated and angry. I threatened to burn down the cell with kerosene and a match, and the *shawisha* hurried off at a run, returning with the Internal Security officer and senior prison administrator.

'My reputation as a nationalist is worth my life to me!' I said angrily. 'I will not stay quiet about this lying, this slander, this defamation of my good name!'

I calmed down only after the Internal Security officer sent off an urgent despatch communicating my protest and my wish to reply to the newspaper.

That night, I did not close my eyes once. What sort of tyrannical oppression was this, practised against us while we were behind bars, lacking a means to reply or defend ourselves?

What crime had been perpetrated against my rights, as an Egyptian woman who had entered prison only because of the stand she had taken and her nationalist writings calling for justice and freedom?

Moreover, what made me even angrier was the fact that I had begun to read articles published in the local newspapers after Sadat's death criticising his policies and calling for a decisive stand to be taken against corruption, injustice, and favouritism. Many words like those which I had published in the age of Sadat and for which I had been imprisoned had now begun to appear in print.

The blood was boiling in my head, and my body was trembling with anger. I grasped my head with my hands. It would be better for me to calm down since I was still behind bars and had no way to defend myself.

Growing slightly calmer, I took a piece of paper and pen and began to write the following letter, addressed to the President of the Republic.

Mr Hosni Mubarak
President of the Republic

Greetings.

Despite my presence in the Barrages Prison I have heard your explanation that the sword of the law will not distinguish between the big and the little. Yet, two crimes have been committed against me, and against the rights which I should enjoy:

1. The first crime was putting me into prison on 6 September 1981 and keeping me there when I have committed no crime except taking a publicly stated position and publishing words in the newspapers defending freedom of opinion, fundamental human rights, and the Egyptian populace. You can confirm this by looking through the report of the investigation which the Socialist Prosecutor ran with me.

2. The second crime consists of the defamation of my reputation as a literary figure and a nationalist. This has taken place while I have been in prison with no means of defending myself or replying to the charges. On the front page of its 23 November 1981 issue, *Al Ahram* newspaper published a false news item which soiled my unblemished reputation as a nationalist. For the benefit of public opinion, it portrays the charges against me as consisting of participation in the implementation of a Soviet blueprint to create chaos in the country. This is the accusation which neither the Internal Security Bureau nor the General Intelligence Bureau dared to direct at me personally.

The impact of these two crimes upon me increases as I read in today's newspapers phrases which are identical to those which I have written previously. These words led to my imprisonment, but today people are competing to write them – just as yesterday they vied to incriminate the same words.

And with all of that, I am still in prison, awaiting release. However, release does not mean merely my departure from prison, but also implementation of the vow which you have obligated yourself to fulfil – for you have stated clearly that you will not promise anything which you are incapable of fulfilling.

For you promised that the sword of the law will not distinguish between big and little. Then, is the sword of the law directed against all who have shared in the two aforementioned crimes? Is it possible for you to return my legal and human rights, and what is my due as a nationalist and literary figure – all of which have been voided for the period of months, weeks, and days?

My nationalist reputation and my honour as a literary person are as valuable to me as my life. I did not inherit them from a father or grandfather, and they have not given me authority or a high position, but I built them up over the years through my struggle and determination, and through them I was able to make my own name: Nawal el Sa'adawi, the Egyptian writer, known – in Egypt, the other Arab nations, and the entire world – for her free pen and her courageous original thinking.

Is it possible for you to fulfil this pledge to which you have bound yourself? I ask you to do so. Thank you. My salutations.

I finished writing the letter as I heard the voice of the curlew. I got up and walked to the door. I jammed my head between the bars, sensing the fresh, moist dawn breeze . . . the morning light creeping in from afar . . . the voice of the curlew resounding, like broken sighs, pleas, sobbing, like a child breathing laughter . . . or crying.

The face of my son appeared, breaking through the darkness, his eyes shining. Behind me, I heard the voices of my *munaqqaba* cellmates . . . the dawn prayer summons, and the ritual prayer.

I put on my sports shoes and began my exercises. The vehement movements relaxed me. The sweat, pouring down thickly, washed away my insomnia and fatigue.

I stuck my head beneath the cold water. Only now did I feel refreshed and hungry, or madly thirsty for a cup of tea.

As soon as I held the hot cup in my hands I heard the key turning in the door . . . and I saw the *ma'mur* standing erect before me. He said, with an irritation which he was suppressing, 'Dr Nawal, pack your bag and come with me.'

I jumped to my feet. 'Where?'

'I don't know.'

'Release?'

'I don't know.'

The cellmates surrounded me. 'It must be release.'

'If it is, why doesn't he say so?' I asked. 'It must be an investigative session or transferral to another prison.'

The *ma'mur* left me to prepare my bag. I was fighting the sensation of joy which I felt at his words. Perhaps it was not release; I might return to prison once again.

But if I were to be coming back to this place, why would he ask me to pack my bag?

I stuffed my clothes into the suitcase. In a small cardboard carton,

I deposited a collection of hair rollers. Never had I rolled my hair in these wire fingers, but in them I had concealed all my papers and the diary entries I'd written each night.

Each of my cellmates hurried to hand me a small letter, whispering in my ear, 'If you get out, send this to my family.'

I hid the letters in my sports shoes, with my letter to the President of the Republic.

I expected them to search me at the door, but no one did so. I saw the great prison doors open to their widest. Everything around me seemed to be running and gasping for breath. Hurriedly, the *ma'mur* gave me the pounds which remained to me in the prison safe, my identity card, and the possessions he had taken from me on the first night I came to prison. Everyone appeared to be in a hurry; the police officers were trying to catch their breath. Their eyes, gazing at me, held an indeterminable look of respect or awe. They led me quickly to a small, private car. I sat in the back. The car took off at a fast pace, gasping and spluttering. Even the driver seemed to be gasping.

I looked around in amazement. 'What's happened?'

'Good news, God willing.'

'Where are you taking me?'

'Good news, God willing.'

'I don't understand anything. What's going on?'

'We are taking you to a specific place.'

'What is this specific place?'

'You'll know when you get there.'

From their manner of talking, I felt that something major had changed. What was it? And what was this new journey towards the unknown? If it was 'good news', as they were saying, why this concealment and suppression? Why would it be a secret trip in this manner?

All my life I have had suspicions about anything which is 'secret'. I cannot bear whispering, concealment, and the failure to face matters squarely.

Why aren't they telling the truth?

I leant my head against the seat back. Two men were sitting in front, one driving and the other gazing at the road. Two completely strange men. I had never seen them before. And the small

Volkswagen, so like a metal box . . . to where was it rushing with this mad haste?

Was this a fast attempt, and a concealed one, to execute me and hide my corpse in the ground?

Was it release? But would release be hidden in this fashion? If so, why?

All sorts of questions were whirling around in my head, raising me to the heights of optimism and joy, then dropping me to the depths of despair and anger: it's my right to know where they are taking me, whether to heaven or hell. I don't much care where I'm going, but I've got to know. I am a human being, not a parcel carried from one place to another. Knowledge is my right. After that, let them take me wherever they wish.

The unfamiliar road always takes on a frightening, even terrifying, aspect – even if paradise lies at its end.

The car was flying over the ground with surprising speed; inside, I was shaking like a feather in a whirlwind. My eyes, observing the streets and people carefully, widened in amazement: I saw a woman walking in the road, swinging her arms with an astounding freedom: it seems she is on her way home? Walking in the street, going home – what marvels! Extraordinary events. Bits of the impossible. How long has it been since I've walked in the street or gone home? 80 years? Maybe, or perhaps it was in another epoch that I did such things . . . another world . . . maybe I've not walked along a street since I was a young child, or a pupil in elementary school.

I noticed a woman driving a car, turning into a side street. And a man entering a grocery shop. How could people move with such simplicity through the streets?

Freedom is a crown which is visible on people's heads only to the one who is imprisoned.

The car stopped before a huge palace. The two men jumped out, and I got out too.

'You are going to meet the President of the Republic now,' said one.

A quick palpitation of the heart. A cautious smile. I was still carrying prison inside, and prison is to doubt what you hear, even if you can see with your own eyes, touch with your own hands, and personally confirm your impressions.

In the elegant reception hall, I saw the faces of thirty individuals who were among those that had been put under precautionary detention. Some of those faces held bewildered looks which suggested that they did not yet believe what they were experiencing. Others were clearly overcome with joy, while still others were reliving the suffering they had sustained.

Their voices embraced, their hearts were pulsing strongly. The light was forceful and brilliant, hurting the exhausted eyes – young eyes and old ones, and eyes that are ageless, as if they are older than time itself and do not grow old or die. The eyes of the simple Egyptian, entering in his dusty shoes and clothes soiled by the dirt of prison to say his piece for posterity.

He stretched out his hand and clasped mine. His hand was open, sincere, frank, direct. Prison vanished, and the doubts within me faded. I had been liberated, and I had grasped my freedom with my own hands. His voice was echoing in my ear. Frank, sincere words which were concise and direct – words that our ears had longed to hear. Justice. Equality. Freedom. Production. Labour. Respect for the divergent opinion. Democracy. An Egypt which is at once Arab and African. The sword of the law does not distinguish between big and little. The war against corruption. Putting an end to the exploitation of the ground-down majority by the privileged minority.

I gave him my letter. He read it through. I raised my hand to request the floor and said what I had to say. I said that the ruler, however upstanding and right-minded, cannot possibly rule on his own as an individual. I said that there always exists a class which isolates the ruler from the people, and transforms the people into a passive majority of onlookers. I said that democracy cannot be achieved without the existence of legal guarantees to protect those with their own opinions from the tyranny of authority. Otherwise, fear will rule the minds of Egyptian men and women.

The meeting ended and we left the hall. I looked around. I believed that they would carry me back to prison, but no one approached me. I walked cautiously towards the outside door. As I was leaving the palace, a journalist stopped me. He was staring at my shoes. 'Sports shoes in Aruba Palace?!!'

'Why are you looking at my shoes, friend? Look at my eyes

instead!' I stepped into the street, carrying my freedom in my eyes like the sunlight.

I stood in the street, bewildered, my suitcase in my hand. People around me were hurrying to accomplish their business, and in a crazed competition the cars raced along the street. No one stopped and looked into my face. It had been a lifetime since I had seen my face in a mirror. Was my appearance as it had been before? Didn't anyone notice the dirt of prison on my features?

I moved my arms and legs; I walked just like the other people. Had I become one of them? Did I belong to this world, and was it possible to get a taxi and go home? Like this, so simply?

I stood motionless for a moment; I placed my bag on the ground. Noticing a taxi approaching, I beckoned to the driver, and the taxi came to a halt.

I got in. 'Giza.' The car moved off. Everything seemed like a dream – Giza Street, as if I had not seen it for a century, and Nile Street, and the bridge. The car pulled on to the verge and stopped. I saw the door to my building, to my home.

I was still moving like a sleepwalker. I pressed my finger on the doorbell. The door opened, and I saw my husband's face.

A moment straight out of a fantasy. It was just like those scenes which take place in stories and novels – from the cell to the Palace of the President of the Republic to the arms of my husband in our own home.

All of this took place on a single morning, that of 25 November 1981. This became the fourth date engraved in my memory, joining 6 October, 6 September, and 28 September.

Four dates, all in the autumn of 1981 and all in Egypt.

My son and daughter returned at three o'clock in the afternoon. I hid myself in order to see them without being seen. I saw their eyes as they gazed towards my empty seat at the table, and my empty bed in the bedroom. A deep, suppressed sadness had transformed the eyes of children into the eyes of old people. Had I seen their eyes – these eyes – in prison, it would have destroyed me. But my brain cells had buried their features in a place unknown to me, and my imagination had been incapable of sketching the sadness in their eyes. I called out to them . . . and it was another moment outside ordinary existence and the world we know. I threw my arms around the two forms which were no longer children's bodies, and the eyes which were no longer children's eyes.

In the embrace, I saw the shine return to the black of the eye, and the childlike quality coming back. With it returned the longing and the desire deposited across 80 years of distance and deep pain, while something in my inner self was saying: 'This stage of my life has ended, and now another one has begun.'

Part VI
The Final Part

I opened my eyes in the morning. No black ceiling. I closed my eyes and opened them again. I did not see the dull grey cracked walls or the steel bars on the door. I shut my eyes again and reopened them. I saw the white bookcase and the rows of books, my picture in a frame next to my husband's picture, and my son's face peering in from the door. I heard my daughter singing in the bath.

I shut my eyes. My voice, singing under the shower, returned to me, as did the hole brimming over with black cockroaches between my feet. I lifted the soft warm blanket from my body and jumped to my feet. My cellmates were still there. In the first release order, only 31 women prisoners had got out, Safinaz and myself among them.

I looked around: the three faces before me, the six eyes surrounding me. I filled my eyes with their features, etching them in my memory. Who knows? Maybe our ways will part. Maybe I'll return to prison. Today, tomorrow, a year from now. Nothing is guaranteed. But prison was no longer that frightening, unknown spectre. My cellmates were still there. I wonder what they're doing right now? And why they have not been freed?

I shut my eyes, and saw them before me, sitting on the dusty ground, faces pale and exhausted, eyes showing anxiety and the effects of insomnia. Feet dirty, soles blackened. My eyes flew open.

'Let's go now!'

'Where?' he asked.

'To the prison.'

It was a peculiar, sudden longing. My husband was not surprised. 'The comradeship of prison is like no other,' he said quietly.

In the car, we reached the Barrages Road. To my right were the expansive green fields and on my left lay the Nile. I recalled the voyage into the unknown which I had made along this same road with the officer at my side and the heads of men and rifles behind me. I turned and looked behind. The cartons of food sat on the back seat, cartons like the containers which he had sent to me every Tuesday.

I shifted my head towards him: his long, slender fingers grasped the steering column; his eyes were fixed to the front. A blend of happiness and sorrow. He turned towards me. I enveloped his hand in mine. 'Every Tuesday, you covered this long distance.'

'Every Tuesday, I thought I would see you.'

I raised my head to the road. The Barrages were behind us now. The car turned of into the side road, and then into the long tunnel-like way. The odour of vegetation and the Nile disappeared, and the smell of dirt filled my nose.

At the end of the tunnel, I saw the long pole blocking the way. The car stopped at the pole, and from the side of the road emerged a thin man, eyes gleaming and darting like the eyes of a highwayman. He hurried over, back stooped, and pulled at the pole, which rose in the air enough to allow the car through, then fell once again and closed the way behind us.

The huge doors opened. There was a welcoming reception – the officials in charge, the warden, and the *shawisha* were all there, eyes shining. Their voices sounded like the pealing of welcoming bells: 'Welcome! welcome! The prison is honoured by your presence. We saw your picture in the papers yesterday with the President of the Republic.'

The *shawisha* bore off the cartons of food to my cellmates and returned, concealing in her bosom a folded slip of paper which I hid in my handbag.

On the way back, I noticed a car coming behind us at a fast clip. Gaining ground, it came to a halt in front of us. My husband stopped the car and we got out. I saw the senior police official, the one with the baton. I imagined that he was going to take me back to prison. However, he approached me with a smile, and whispered in my ear.

'If you meet the President's deputy, Mr Nabawi Ismail, mention my name. I have a promotion coming which is overdue.'

He got back into his car and moved off quickly.

The blood must have drained from my face, for my husband looked at me and inquired, 'What was that about?' Bewildered, I told him. 'Can you believe it?'

'Yes, I can,' he replied calmly.

I opened my handbag and read what was written on the bit of folded paper. 'Try as hard as you can to get the doctors to transfer us to Qasr el Aini or Demerdash Hospital.'

We went straight to the College of Medicine at Ain Shams University. Our physician colleagues recoiled; all but one abstained from offering help. That exception was chairperson of the Department of Mental Diseases. He emptied a departmental room for the prisoners, and the next day they were moved from the prison to that room. After a few more days, an order for their release – all of them – was issued.

The days and the occupations of life separated us. As soon as I meet one of them anywhere at all, though, we embrace and remember the days of prison – as if there is something about prison which one misses, or as if the comradeship of prison cannot be forgotten and cannot die. And who knows, perhaps it will return.